DEAR ANDREW:

Letters and Memoirs of a Holocaust Survivor to His Grandson

By Andrew Ross & Deborah Erna Oury

www.ten16press.com - Waukesha, WI

Dear Andrew: Letters and Memoirs of a Holocaust Survivor to His Grandson
Copyrighted © 2017 Deborah Erna Oury
ISBN 978-1-943331-61-1
Library of Congress Control Number: 2017909666
Cover design by Kaeley Dunteman

All Rights Reserved. Written permission must be secured from the publisher to use or reproduce any part of this book, except for brief quotations in critical reviews or articles.

For information, please contact:

www.ten16press.com
Waukesha, WI

The author has made every effort to ensure that the information within this book was accurate at the time of publication. The author does not assume and hereby disclaims any liability to any party for any loss, damage, or disruption caused by errors or omissions, whether such errors or omissions result from accident, negligence, or any other cause.

"For the survivor who chooses to testify, it is clear; his duty is to bear witness for the dead and for the living. He has no right to deprive future generations of a past that belongs to our collected memory. To forget would be not only dangerous but offensive; to forget the dead would be akin to killing a second time."

-Eli Wiesel in *Night*

INTRODUCTION

Since my childhood, I have known that my dad was a Holocaust survivor. Having my grandmother's name as my middle name made me think often of her horrific death.

I knew my dad had a story to tell. Over the years, he dropped bits and pieces, which only made me all the more curious about the gaps in between.

When Hollywood movie director, Steven Spielberg, and his Shoah Foundation started recording survivors' stories, I urged my dad to tell his. He replied that he had worked so hard to forget. Revisiting that part of his experience would be like pulling scabs from wounds that were trying to heal.

He had not forgotten though. Each year at Yom Kippur (Jewish Day of Atonement) as he lit the yahrzeit candles for his loved ones who were no longer with us, his tears would flow.

When my oldest son returned home on summer break from the United States Air Force Academy in Colorado, he handed me a stack of envelopes containing letters from his grandpa. "You may want to keep these in a safe place. They are all about Grandpa's history," he advised.

I started opening and eagerly reading each one. I read in fascination as his long awaited story started to unfold.

In my dad's eighty-ninth year, with the letters to my son as a starting point, he finally began to tell his whole story. The gaps were filled in.

The following pages contain the story of one unique Holocaust survivor among thousands, and we hope it serves as a memorial to millions.

Deborah Erna Oury

PREFACE

A proud grandpa gathered with family and friends to celebrate his grandson's acceptance into the United States Air Force Academy in Colorado Springs, Colorado.

On a glorious Wisconsin spring day, he watched as the Air Force Liaison officer handed his grandson the formal looking Certificate of Acceptance. The Lieutenant Colonel explained Basic Cadet Training (BCT pronounced "Beast") that would mark his grandson's entry into the Air Force Academy would be grueling. Besides pushing the incoming cadets or "Doolies" to their physical and emotional limits, they would also have no communication with the outside world for weeks and weeks except for U.S. Mail, "snail mail." "Please send your 'Doolie' lots of mail to show encouragement and support," requested the Lieutenant Colonel.

The loving grandpa began a letter writing campaign that continued throughout his grandson's first year at the Academy. The letters contained encouragement, wisdom, observations, and life experiences that the grandpa shared with his oldest grandson who was leaving home and heading out into the world on his own. This grandson's very existence was a miracle. Decades earlier, when the grandpa was just seventeen, he was a Hungarian Jew caught in Hitler's hell, trying to escape the Nazis' extermination machine.

PART 1: RESILIENCE

RESILIENCE
September 11, 2009

Dear Andrew,

I cannot tell you how happy I was when I saw you [at Parents Weekend] and also noticed how well, how easily you adapted to this "strange" environment. The adjustment from sea level to over seven thousand feet above at the Air Force Academy is difficult. I'm using this image in a much greater context. As you will experience, not all can make such drastic changes easily or at all. The key word here is RESILIENCE, and you got it! Resilience separates the men from the boys, the strong from the weak, the survivor from the fallen. Perhaps this was your first real test to find out if you were resilient. I'm happy to see that you passed the test with flying colors. There will be many more I assure you. Now that you passed the first and difficult one, you can be confident that you can pass them all with grace and style. The Nazis, who were determined to kill me, provided me with my first resilience test. The stakes were high: you fail, you die! After that big one, all my life's tests were gentler. I knew that I could handle them with confidence.

My congratulations to you for having passed the first BIGGIE so well, Andrew. YOU GOT WHAT IT TAKES! I am proud of you!

I love you, Grandpa

UNCLE BÉLA AND AUNT SOPHIE
September 20, 2009

Dear Andrew,

"Endre, Uncle Béla and Aunt Sophie are coming by today to say goodbye," my mother broke the news gently with a hint of sadness in her voice. The year was 1941. My Uncle Béla and Aunt Sophie Rosenthal were leaving by train the next day for Portugal. From there they hoped to catch a boat to America. Portugal was the only neutral country left where trans-Atlantic shipping was still possible. Consequently, thousands upon thousands of refugees from Nazi-occupied lands were converging upon Portugal to escape Europe.

It was not an easy decision for my Uncle Béla to leave Hungary. Although he was only in his thirties, he had built the foremost fashion house in Budapest. His spring and fall shows were attended by the famous and high class ladies in Budapest, Prague, and Vienna. His salon was situated in an 18th century palace with tall windows overlooking the central square in Budapest. The elegant interior boasted pigeon-gray carpet and chocolate-brown sofas. Some sixty seamstresses, three cutters, and a dozen models were busy six days a week. It was always an exciting place for me to visit. Amidst all the constant activity, Uncle Béla was always happy to see me, his only nephew.

Aunt Sophie's two older brothers were living in New York. They had left Hungary in 1914 just before the outbreak of

World War I choosing not to serve in the Austro-Hungarian Army. Now in 1941, it just so happened that they had sent their mother a steamship ticket to come to New York. While visiting her sons, she had become deathly ill. The brothers immediately notified their sister Sophie telling her she should come at once if she wanted to see her mother before she died. As the only daughter, she and her mother were very close, so she desperately wanted to get to America. [Unfortunately, her mother passed during Aunt Sophie's voyage].

It was a tearful farewell all around. Uncle Béla was leaving behind his sick mother, paralyzed by a stroke, his sister, his brother-in-law, and his fourteen-year-old nephew. It weighed heavy on his mind that Hitler, who had invaded Vienna, Austria, in 1938, was less than two hundred miles from Budapest, a little too close for comfort. It was true that many believed Hitler would leave Hungary alone as they had been such good allies in World War I. My father, who had been a highly-decorated Ranger officer fighting alongside the Germans for five years, reasoned as well that Germany would respect Hungary's friendship.

In the midst of the tears, kisses, and goodbyes, Uncle Béla stopped for a moment and very quietly said, "When the war is over, I will send for Endre. I want him to come to America."

Germany did leave Hungary alone, for three more years. And then…

Love, Grandpa

INVASION
October 11, 2009

Dear Andrew,

No one, I repeat no one, expected the Germans to invade Hungary in March 1944. For one thing, Hungary was a strong, loyal ally of the Nazis. The Axis nations consisted of Germany, Italy, Japan, and the junior partner, Hungary. Spain was a sympathetic friend of the Germans, but President Franco remained neutral throughout the war. The Germans did not invade Spain.[1]

Hungary sent tens of thousands of soldiers to the Russian front to fight alongside the Germans just as they had done in the First World War. Thousands died in the east. But the Jews were the big problem [for Hitler] in Hungary. The Hungarian Regent, Admiral Miklos Horthy[2], knew that the Germans were totally crazed with the idea of killing each and every Jew in Europe, but he was not going to be a party to this lunacy. Don't get the impression that Horthy was in love with the Jews. The opposite was true. He wildly disliked the Jews, but he was not crazy.

---

[1] "In 1933, approximately 9.5 million Jews lived in Europe...This number represented more than 60 percent of the world's Jewish population...Poland with about 3,000,000 Jews...Germany with about 525,000...Romania with about 756,000...Hungary with 445,000 [This number went up drastically as Jewish refugees fled to Hungary, one of the last Nazi holdouts]...4,000 in Spain [Many Sephardic Jews fled Spain in 1492 during the Spanish Inquisition. Endre's ancestors were among them]" (The United States Holocaust Memorial Museum, "Jewish Population").

[2] Although Hungary is a land-locked country, during the First World War, Horthy was Admiral of the Austro-Hungarian Imperial Navy on the Adriatic Sea. After the war, the Hapsburg monarchy, which was openly friendly to the Jews, was deposed and the Austro-Hungarian Empire ceased to exist (Lambert, "The Horthy Era").

There was another reason why Hungary felt secure from a German invasion. In 1944, everyone in Europe knew that the Allies were grouping a gigantic force in Britain in preparation for crossing the English Channel and attacking Germany. It was reasoned that the Germans would concentrate all their efforts, and devote all their assets, to protect the coast and force the Allied invaders back into the sea.

Since when did reason play a role in Hitler's thinking? Hitler did want to win the war, of course, but the war was only of secondary importance. The main thing, and most important goal in his life, was to totally eradicate the Jews. He saw the Jews as a curse to humanity. The Jews would contaminate the superior white race; therefore, he would be the instrument that would prevent that from ever happening. Hitler saw himself as the savior of the purity of the Aryan race.

Heinrich Himmler, the chief executioner of the Jews, was buzzing in Hitler's ears that Admiral Horthy was sabotaging the noble cause and arrogantly defying Hitler's wishes by trying to protect Hungary's nearly one million Jews. Hitler lost his patience and ordered a halt to the shipping of tanks, guns, and ammunition to the coast. Instead he ordered several divisions be sent to Hungary to get rid of that Jew-loving Hungarian government. On March 19, 1944, the gates at the border were smashed, and German troops poured into Hungary. Admiral Horthy was deposed, eventually arrested, and exiled to Portugal. A new Nazi government, the Arrow Cross party, was put in control. Anti-Jewish regulations were announced daily: Jews must move to Yellow-Star buildings, all

Jews must wear a yellow star, Jews may only leave their homes between 10 a.m.-12 p.m., etc.

Here is an interesting thought. Because Hitler diverted precious war effort resources and wasted time concentrating on the Hungarian Jewish problem, did he weaken his resistance at the coast and make the Allies' landing more doable as a result?[3] The Invasion of Normandy was not easy, but it was successful.

Love, Grandpa

---

[3] Hitler's mismanagement of the war resulted in a few of his top military officials' attempt to assassinate him. On July 20, 1944, Colonel Claus von Stauffenberg placed a briefcase containing a bomb next to Hitler while he was sitting at his conference table in his Wolf's Lair field headquarters. Someone unknowingly moved the briefcase so when the blast occurred, Hitler suffered only minor injuries. Had the plot succeeded in July 1944, countless Jewish lives would have been saved, including Endre's parents Josef and Erna ("Claus Von Stauffenberg").

FINAL FAREWELL
October 17, 2009

Dear Andrew,

October 19, 1944, will be a date I will remember forever. On this day, the Hungarian Arrow Cross (Nazis) burst into our building. Running from apartment to apartment, they went about rounding up able-bodied men to transport to a Labor Camp. They announced that they were taking men to help construct tank traps to slow the oncoming Russian Army. Our four-story apartment building, marked with the Star of David, was in a turmoil. Amidst a lot of yelling, screaming, and cursing, the young hate-filled troops assembled about fifty Jewish men in our courtyard.

"Mama," I said to my sweet, beautiful, loving mother who kept quietly weeping, "You know the war is practically over. The Russians are only sixty kilometers (forty miles) from Budapest. By next week, these Nazi thugs will be hanging from elm trees on Andrassy Boulevard. Please don't cry."

"Erna," my father chimed in, "I am certain that whatever comes, Endre will survive. He's a lot smarter than these Nazi thugs."

My mother stopped weeping and gave me a little, forced smile. "Take care of yourself, my dear son. I will always love you."

My Uncle Sándor Lustig and I were taken by force from the apartment. As the Nazis lined us up against the wall facing our apartment in the courtyard and started to march us away, I looked up to see my mother, father, and my mother's cousin, Sándorné Lustig, all standing at the window, anxiously watching us.

I will never forget the look on my mother's face. That picture of her is vivid in my memory, as if it happened yesterday. A mixture of fear, sadness, and horror is what I saw. It was as if she knew that this was the last time she would see me.

I was somewhat puzzled by what I saw in her face. Being young and always optimistic, I assumed that we would leave for a few days, and when we finished building the tank traps, we would all come back home.

Together we were marched to a nearby park where hundreds of Jews wearing yellow stars were already assembled. There was a lot of shouting, cursing, rifle butting, kicking, and punching. Welcome to Nazi paradise! They formed us into columns of five and slowly marched us from the center of Budapest toward the outskirts of town. By the end of the day, we were marched onto the field of a big soccer stadium. A very wet snow had started to fall. I tried to cover myself by draping my coat over my head and rolling up into a little ball on the wet grass. It was a rather futile attempt to stay warm and dry. All through the long night, I kept telling myself that this was a Boy Scout campout. My coat was the tent, and come tomorrow the ordeal would be over and we would all be going back home. The Nazis had plans for us which definitely did not include going home.

The next day, in our frozen stiff condition, the march

resumed toward a new destination. There was nothing to eat but I did not mind much because my severe discomfort was a distraction. After several hours of marching through streets lined with gawking, jeering, and cursing Hungarians (all the while wondering what I did to these people that they hated me so much), we finally arrived at an abandoned quarry. This was a considerable improvement because we now had a roof over our heads. There was no heat so we were still cold but at least it was dry. They gave us some thin, watery soup which did nothing to stop our hunger, but it did warm us up a bit. We had arrived at a labor camp.[4]

Miraculously, after a few days at the quarry, a Christian neighbor lady showed up with a package from my mother! I don't know how my parents found out where I was nor how they managed to find the food they scraped together to send me. A note with words of encouragement from both my mother and father was inside the package. They urged me to stay brave, never to give up, and to hold on for a better, brighter future.

I still have this note with my parents' last words. Knowing that my mother and father touched it, and probably kissed it before sending it to me, makes me cry every time I hold it.

Love, Grandpa

---

[4] "Jewish labor battalions...had to suffer from horrendous living and internment conditions similar to those in the concentration camps of the S.S." ("The Holocaust: Forced Labor").

BOY SCOUTS

As an only child growing up in Budapest in the 1930s and 1940s, I was always more comfortable with adults than with children my own age. I did have three boy cousins with whom I often played, and one very good friend from school, Tibor Garai, whom I met in fourth grade.

When we were eleven, Tibor announced that he was joining Boy Scouts and suggested that I should do the same. When I mentioned this at home, my grandmother immediately jumped on the idea and insisted I should do it. There was no denying my grandmother, so I told Tibor I would like to accompany him to his next meeting.

Boy Scouting was fairly new. It was just thirty years old when I joined. Scouting was driven by the boys [and there was] very little parental involvement as it is now. The reason was that we were not dependent on our parents to drive us here or there. We depended on public transportation. For instance, in summer months, we frequently went camping in the Budapest hills and forests. For a nickel, we took the Number 6 streetcar to the Cogwheel train terminal, and for a dime, the Cogwheel train took us to the top of János Hegy (John Mountain). In the wintertime, we took the Cogwheel train to go skiing.

My friend Tibor joined Boy Scout Troop 310 Jókai Mór. It

was a Jewish troop which meant that a synagogue sponsored it. Otherwise, there was no religious influence. As a matter of fact, the name Jókai Mór was not a Jewish name, but the name of a very famous Hungarian writer and poet. By comparison, the Christian-sponsored Boy Scout troops were deeply religious.

Our troop consisted of three platoons of thirty to thirty-five boys, and two adult leaders: the Scoutmaster and the treasurer. We called the adults "Unc" for uncle.

I started out at age eleven on the bottom, but two years later, I was "trail" leader overseeing eight boys. By the time I was fifteen, I was a platoon leader of over thirty boys. Needless to say, I loved every minute of it.

We went on frequent weekend camping trips, weather permitting. That is when we worked toward earning merit badges and survival skills. We often played "war" by attaching a number to the front of our Canadian Mountie-styled hats. The objective was to "kill" the enemy by crawling close enough to be able to see his number without being seen yourself. When you would shout out his number, he would be "dead." It wasn't an easy game. You had to learn to hide behind bushes or in ditches, and you had to practice a long time to become "invisible." This ability to blend into my environment helped me later, during the time of Nazi occupation.

We weren't allowed to bring prepared food to campouts. We had to cook our meals from scratch. This was another survival challenge, because some of the stuff those boys cooked was really hard to swallow. We learned to eat everything prepared, no matter how disgusting it was. This too, helped me when I was on the run from the Nazis. The most frequent menu item was boiled potatoes with tomato sauce. The potatoes were always burnt or half raw but we ate them anyway.

The competition to earn more and more merit badges was fierce. My platoon did a great job, notwithstanding frequent accidents and medical problems that were unavoidable among so many rambunctious boys. One boy broke his back falling into a deep hole and was kept in a body cast for six months. I had to pick up his homework and help with his assignments every day for six months!

Once a year, we took the train and went to Jamboree, where we met Boy Scout troops from all over [Hungary]. We exchanged small gifts, made new friends, and promised to visit each other. I actually got an invitation from a boy from Pécs and went for three days. Unfortunately, I got sick as a dog, and spent the entire three days in my friend's bathroom. What a visit!

As the boys grew older and developed an interest in girls, they started to lose interest in scouting. What a shame! Seeing the inevitable, I asked my girlfriend Zsuzsi Munk, if she would mind starting a Girl Scout troop. She said she would, and so we went hiking with the girls (but not camping). My boys were now eager to come to scouts, and I did not have any absenteeism from my platoon.

The Nazi Era was deadly to our troop. The number of boys that were killed was absolutely heartbreaking. If you figure that we had roughly one hundred members, only four of us survived of whom I know. They were my boyhood friend, Dr.

Tibor Garai, a Hungarian Phd. in Chemistry; Leslie Schnée, a Canadian restaurateur; Péter Orosz, Israeli Secret Service (now deceased); and myself. All the others, including the two adults, perished.

    I often think about them and try to recollect their young faces, their mischiefs, their pleasure when they earned another merit badge, their playfulness, their beautiful young lives. The older I get, the more I miss them. I have no desire to go back and visit our old camp grounds. I cry just thinking about them. Perhaps we will meet again in the not too distant future.

THE GETAWAY
October 30, 2009

Dear Andrew,

We were building tank traps. We woke before dawn to dig up cobblestones on the streets, then built small ragged hills that were supposed to stop or slow down Soviet tanks. They [tank traps] looked ineffective but those lumbering Soviet tanks were not on the move anyway. Much to our distress when every day or even every hour made the difference between life and death, those Soviet tanks [offering liberation for the Jews] were firmly parked about sixty kilometers from Budapest. In the evening, when we returned to the quarry, we were given our one meal for the day: a bowl of watery soup with scraps of carrots and cabbage thrown in.

On October 29, 1944, after waking us early in the morning, the routine was different. Instead of lining us up for tank trap work, the Nazis ordered us to pack our stuff (what stuff?), for we were going to leave. Where to? No one would say. Fifteen minutes later we were marching in our columns of five. My Uncle Sándor was standing next to me. I was working secretly to loosen the yellow star on my breast pocket because I was determined that I was not going to march with these damn Nazis. I had seen enough to know they had nothing nice planned for me.

"Uncle," I said, "When the moment is right, I'm going to escape from this column."

"No, Endre," my Uncle Sándor pleaded, "Don't do it. The Nazis are shooting would-be escapists on the streets. And it's daylight, making it much too risky."

"I promise to watch my step and will wait until I don't attract attention," I insisted.

The columns started to move. Armed Nazi guards marched with us on both sides of the column. Rain mixed with snow and a fierce wind worked in my favor as we marched west on the big boulevard toward the Danube River which separated Buda (west) from Pest (east). We came to the Elizabeth Bridge, an old, very ornate, elegant bridge. Traffic halted as we marched on the wide roadway. Elizabeth Bridge had pedestrian walkways on both sides with only two benches spread apart on each side. When we walked by the first bench a guard was near me so I marched on. However, when we got to the second bench, the guard, with his head hunched into his coat as far as it would go, had walked ahead of me so I decided the time was now. I ripped off my yellow star and jammed it into my pocket. Saying goodbye to my uncle, I stepped swiftly to the right, and as the column moved forward, I sat down. I watched column after column of people marching by, [trying to look like an interested bystander] with a curious look on my face, all the while holding my breath. Why would a casual observer want to sit on a bench in such nasty weather? Anybody looking at me would immediately discover I didn't belong there. But no one looked. Afraid to move, [and] with a silly, frozen smile on my face, I sat like a statue. Why can't they move faster? How many guards will march by without becoming suspicious of this character sitting in the cold on the bridge's bench? Miraculously, no one gave me a second look. After the last column marched off, I continued to sit a little longer and then stood up to leave. But where could I go? Where could I hide?

I was in a precarious position. I needed to get off the bridge as quickly as possible without attracting attention to myself, and I needed to find a hiding place where I could disappear. The Russians were only sixty kilometers away, and if they started to move, they could be in Budapest in a day. I just needed to buy some time. I got up and started casually walking toward the east, Pest, thinking how odd I must look to be walking in the cold, wet weather on a Danube bridge of all places.

As soon as I got off the bridge, I decided to go back to my apartment and let my mom and dad know I was okay. I rushed back to the building and up the stairs to our apartment only to find it was locked! My knocking disturbed our Christian neighbor.

"Oh, Endre," she exclaimed, "You are back. The Nazis came a few hours ago and took your parents along with all the rest of the Jews. I have no idea where," with that she quickly closed her door.

Now what? Two doors down from our apartment lived a Jewish family. Mr. and Mrs. Winkler and their eight-year-old daughter, Marika, were friends with my family. Mr. Winkler owned a fruit and vegetable store just down the street from our building. Lou Winkler was built like a prize fighter from lifting hundred pound boxes of fruits and vegetables all day long. He was a handsome guy in his early thirties with an insanely jealous wife.

"Lou, why do you take your lady customers' hands and massage them when they come to buy lettuce?" she would ask obviously unhappy.

"Sweetheart," he would reply, "There are two other vegetable stores on the same block. Do they come to my store and buy from me because my lettuce tastes or smells better than the competitions'? No, they buy from me because I am friendly and flirt a little."

Mrs. Winkler tried to accept his logic but she was never quite satisfied.

Because he was of military age, Lou Winkler was drafted into the Hungarian Work Brigade for Jewish men. The brigade was basically slave labor for the Hungarian military. Lou had pulled off his yellow star to sneak back home to see his wife and daughter, but they had also just been taken when he ran into me.

"What are you doing here?" he asked. "The Nazis could come back here at any minute, and it would be very dangerous for you if they found you here."

"I agree," was my reply, "But I don't have the vaguest idea where to go and hide."

"Well," he said thoughtfully, "Maybe I can smuggle you into my brigade. They have no roster, no organization and no structure. We're just a bunch of Jewish men doing slave labor with the Hungarian military guarding us. They'll never notice you don't belong there."

"Great," I exclaimed with relief, "Let's go, and I'll try to make like ashes on a gray rug."

I was very grateful to Lou for helping me find a place to hide for a while as I expected the Russians to occupy Budapest within days. That evening we snuck into a bombed-out school building that housed the brigade. After a meal of some thin soup, the men made room for me to lie down on my overcoat on the floor and the lights went out. What would tomorrow morning bring?

Love, Grandpa

THE POLGÁR FAMILY

Before I was taken away to Labor Camp, I was a seventeen-year-old boy living with my mother, father, my mother's cousin and her husband, Uncle Sándor and Aunt Sándorné Lustig. We five had to share one room and a kitchen. The communal toilet was at the end of the courtyard. The reason we all lived in this four-story apartment building in the center of Budapest was because it was a Yellow-Star building, where Jews were forced to move in 1944[5]. There was a yellow star prominently placed above the front entrance doors.

It didn't take long for the Hungarian Nazis, called the Arrow Cross, to start making life miserable for the Jews. Only a few days after German occupation, the first bomb-shell was Jews had to deliver all their radios to such and such collection place. This was bad for us because radios were our only link to the outside world and reliable news. Hungarian newspapers were full of Nazi lies, and only the BBC (British Broadcasting Company) was accurate. Next, came the other blow: Jews had to surrender all cars, motorcycles, and even bicycles to the government. I had to deliver my red and chrome bike to a

---
[5] "On 16 June, 1944, the mayor of Budapest, Ákos Dorogi Farkas, issued a decree that marked out almost 2,000 apartment buildings in Budapest 'in which Jews...may reside.' Everyone of these apartment buildings had to 'mark all their street entrances with a yellow star...' According to the 1941 census, almost 21 percent of Budapest's population was of Jewish origin. The order to wear the yellow star therefore applied to 187,000 Jews." (www.yellowstarhouses.org)

suburban soccer field and get a receipt for it. That was painful as that bike was my prized possession. Soon after, Jews had to move into Yellow-Star houses. Then came the curfew. We were only allowed to leave the building for three hours a day. We could be shot if we were found on the street before or after "open door." Shopping for food became more and more difficult. We only had a couple of hours a day that we could leave our homes, so the lines at the stores became longer and longer, and one could buy less and less in the allotted time.

The Arrow Cross took over the police and all important government functions. They [Hungarian Arrow Cross] not only obeyed the Germans' orders to treat the Jews inhumanely, but exceeded even the Germans in their cruelty and bloodthirstiness.

On the fourth floor of our apartment building, in the corner apartment, was the home of the Polgár family. They were Mr. and Mrs. Polgár and their two lovely, young daughters, ages eight and ten.

Mr. Polgár was a genuine V.I.P. because he was the station master of the Hungarian National Railways Budapest "West" Terminal (Nyugati). The "West" was not the main rail terminal in Budapest. It was second to the "East" (Keleti). Nevertheless, the "West" was a busy, important terminal with many thousands of passengers daily.

Because Mr. Polgár didn't have any sons, he took a liking to me. He introduced me to railroading. The two most important functions were switching trains and the coupling and uncoupling of train cars. In those days, these tasks had to be done by hand. It was difficult and dangerous work. Mr. Polgár continuously trained workers in safety. He was proud of the fact that under his watch the "West" never had a single serious injury.

While the technology interested me, I was more excited by people watching: the energy and movements of people, and the personalities of different trains.

The trains had a distinct pecking order. At the very bottom were the commuter trains. These were no frill, bare bottom trains, just slightly better than ordinary streetcars because they had toilets. They all had wooden benches and only carried third class. These trains came in the morning bringing the commuters to the capital city. After they discharged their passengers, they were pulled out of the station and parked for the day in outside "graveyards." In the evening, they were back to take the suburbanites to their homes.

One step above the commuter trains were the Outer-urban trains. These were long distance trains connecting Budapest with major Hungarian cities. Budapest-Pécs, Budapest-Debrecen, and Budapest-Győr were some of the routes. These trains had a lot more comfort. They had dining cars and three classes of compartments. Sometimes they even had a parlor car, depending on the distance they traveled.

After this came train aristocracy; the outer-continental trains, Budapest-Paris, Budapest-Berlin, Budapest-Rome, and Budapest-Warsaw were some of the routes. These were luxurious, long-distance trains. They had sleeping cars (bunk beds or private compartments), dining cars, snack cars, parlor cars, and even piano entertainment. Trips could take several days to cross the continent.

And then there was train royalty, none other than The Orient Express! The Orient Express would leave Paris' Gare Saint-Lazare on Tuesday at 3 p.m. It crossed eastern France and headed into Italy for the first stop in Venice. After a short layover, it continued east to Vienna, Austria. From there, just a short hop to Budapest arriving Thursday at 7 p.m. Then, it turned south through the Balkans, stopping at Belgrade, Yugoslavia, Athens, Greece, and arriving at its final destination, Istanbul, Turkey, on Saturday at 1 p.m.

The arrival of The Orient Express in Budapest always created a great deal of excitement. Sometime before its arrival, visitors welcoming passengers would jam the platform. Passengers waiting to board the train for the southern portion of the trip would mill eagerly. Baggage handlers would push their wooden carts close to where the baggage car would stop. Vendors of newspapers and magazines would noisily hawk their wares. The excitement would rise until suddenly the commotion quieted. That is when Mr. Polgár would make the awaited announcement:

"Attention, Attention! The Orient Express is now approaching the terminal. It will arrive shortly on Track Number 1. Please, everyone on the platform, step back as far from the edge as you can, for your own safety! Thank you very much."

Pretty soon, the vibration could be felt underfoot. The Orient Express was nearing, pulled by two gigantic steam locomotives. Bells ringing and spot lights shining, the train slowly rolled into the station. All twelve blue and gold cars projected elegance: a Ritz Hotel on wheels. It was a truly magnificent train. I would look inside the compartments where the shades were pulled up. Small table lamps on pull down tables, golden yellow shades, all well-dressed passengers, uniformed waiters scurrying inside: pure luxury. Oh, it was all so exciting, so colorful! Ticket prices were so high only well-heeled people could afford to travel in this style from Paris to Istanbul.

But Mr. Polgár had a big problem. He was a Jew.

However, the mitigating circumstance, and what allowed him to continue to be Station Master, was that his wife was Christian and his two daughters were only half Jewish. That is why, when the Nazis occupied Hungary in March 1944, he was a so-called "privileged" Jew who was entitled to wear a white Star of David instead of the hated yellow regulation star.

Being a "privileged" Jew was a big plus for all of us. When the Nazis introduced curfew for all Jewish tenants, Mr. Polgár was free to leave the building to pick up medicine for anyone who needed it in an emergency, or to make special trips and errands when necessary.

All of this ended on October 29, 1944 when the Nazis planned to make a "clean sweep." By the end of the day, they expected Budapest to be free of Jews. All thought Mr. Polgár was safe. However, there was a loud banging on the door of the Polgár apartment.

"All Jews come out and assemble in the courtyard!"

A cadre of young Nazi Party thugs, armed and boisterous, were herding Jewish families from their apartments. The Polgár front door opened with a bang and Mrs. Polgár, with eyes blazing, shouted at the Nazis," What do you want here, punks?"

The Nazi leader replied," We're here to collect the filthy Jew named Polgár!"

"Are you blind?" shouted Mrs. Polgár. "Don't you see that Mr. Polgár is wearing a white star because he is a 'privileged' Jew? Get out of here before I call my friend the police chief, and you will have to apologize for your insolence!"

"Lady, you are behind the times. Last week, they stopped this 'privileged' Jew nonsense. From now on, a Jew is a filthy Jew, whether he wears a yellow star, purple star, or white star," stated the Nazi.

"If what you are saying is true," said Mrs. Polgár, "And you insist on taking Mr. Polgár with you, we are all going with him. This family, the Polgár family, will not be separated. Where one goes, we all go." With that, she turned to the two little girls who were huddling in the corner of the room scared to death, "Girls!"

"Yes, Mama," replied the older.

"I want you to pack your small suitcases, only with essentials. Pack light. We don't want anything heavy. We will be back in a couple of days, so there is no need for a bunch of stuff."

"Yes, Mama," said the older one, and they scurried into their bedroom for their things.

"Lady, you are completely crazy," said the Nazi leader. "I don't know where they are taking these Jews, but I guarantee you, it is not a country club. If one doesn't have to go, by all means, one should not go. We have orders to take the Jew Polgár. No one said anything about taking the family. Forget this nonsense to go with the Jew. You are risking your and your daughters' lives. Come to your senses!"

Mrs. Polgár just looked at him and in a much quieter tone replied, "Punk, you don't know anything about loyalty, about family, about love. You're so ignorant. We Polgárs belong together. Where one goes, we all go. You Nazis only understand hatred. We, on the other hand, only understand love!"

"Suit yourself," he answered, "Don't say I did not warn you."

At this point, the two little girls appeared, with small suitcases, and their hats and coats on. They all decided to go with their dad, to share his fate, whatever that might be. Mr. and Mrs. Polgár dressed for the chilly, fall October day, and all four Polgárs descended to the courtyard. None of them ever returned to the apartment at Eötvos Utca 35 in Budapest.

A few fortunate people made it back; they survived the camps. Some seemed to have spotted the Polgárs at Mauthausen Camp in Austria. Some others were sure that they had seen them at Auschwitz. They were probably both right. Many Budapest Jews were transported to Mauthausen first. Then, because the camp was completely filled, many were relocated to Auschwitz, where bigger gas chambers and bigger furnaces were "processing" executions faster. Mr. and Mrs. Polgár and their daughters needlessly perished in the Nazi gas chambers.

The apartment on the fourth floor was eventually allocated to a Hungarian family with two children. They received all the belongings of the Polgárs: furniture, silverware, clothing, and souvenirs.

Mr. Polgár broadened my horizons. He allowed me to think of far away, exotic places that a young boy dreamed about reaching one day. He was the person who helped me understand that Budapest was just a small point on the map and made me wish for big, beautiful, faraway places like New York.

Hitler and the Nazis succeeded in eliminating the Polgárs and millions of Jews from the face of the earth. I write this as a remembrance of the Polgár family so that the Nazis do not succeed in extinguishing their memory. They may have been killed in 1944 or 1945, but they will live on in my heart for the rest of my life.

In the sixty-five years since emigrating to America, I have only returned five times to Budapest. But each time, I made my pilgrimage to Budapest "West." I climbed up on the balcony where Mr. Polgár used to supervise the activities. I placed a little bouquet of flowers on the bench and said Kaddish, the Jewish prayer for the dead, for each of them.

The terminal building was the same as I remembered it. However, there were a few changes to the inside. The big steam locomotives are gone. Now, all the engines are diesel driven. Also, the wooden, push-type baggage carts have been replaced by battery powered electric carts. They make less noise, but do a lot of toot-tooting. The main change was the automation of the two dangerous activities: switching and coupling. A control room on the second floor was added for all the computers. Now, the only people on the tracks are the wheel pounders who are looking for cracks. Traffic was much lighter than it was in the old days. Airplanes have taken most of the passengers away from the railroads. The intercontinental lines are especially emptier, as long distance travel is done mostly by plane. The inter-city lines were still fairly busy. Trains are a good way to travel within Hungary.

As I stood on the balcony, I tried to remember the happy feeling I had as a child standing next to Mr. Polgár observing the scene below. I tried to remember the excitement, the sounds, the smell of steam engines, and the din created by the passengers. As I looked down the track and watched the comings and goings, I suddenly believed I heard the announcement in Mr. Polgár's studied calm voice:

"Attention, attention! The Orient Express is now approaching the terminal. It will arrive shortly on Track Number 1. For your own safety, please step back from the edge of the platform. Thank you very much!"

ESCAPE!
October 30, 2009

Dear Andrew,

Life on the brigade became fairly routine. We worked all day building tank traps, fortifications—busy work mainly. Our treatment by the professional Hungarian soldiers was impersonal. These soldiers were not the fanatic, murderous Hungarian Nazi Arrow Cross, but regular military personnel. This was okay but for how long? I had learned by now to expect the worst, so Lou Winkler and I saved some foodstuffs that he had been able to collect from his store. One can of lard, one jar of preserves, and some crackers were the treasures we kept stuffed in our coat pockets. Meanwhile, the Russians who were parked outside of Budapest did some occasional bombing but no troop movements at all. What were they waiting for?

Our routine was suddenly shattered early one morning while it was still dark. "Get up! Get up!" was the wakeup call shouted all over the school building. "Hurry up and get downstairs," they screamed at us in the dark. People were dressing quickly and running in a stampede down the staircase toward the street level. Grabbing Lou by the arm, I whispered, "We are going upstairs, not downstairs. Who knows where they are taking us." Lou readily agreed and so with this thought in our minds, we started to climb up the stairs pushing and shoving against the stream of humanity. People looked at us with surprise as if they were thinking, "What are those two idiots doing climbing up to what and where?" The question was not without merit because as we climbed up toward the top floor, we discovered the roof had been blown off the building leaving only naked rafters, beyond which was the starry sky. We were in trouble. Suddenly, I discovered a two-story water tower sticking up in the air and a long ladder leading up to it. "Hurry, Lou," I cried, "Let's climb up and hide there." Lou and I climbed up, then pulled the ladder up to the tower so there was no way to get to us. The only hazard up there were the broken roof tiles. The blast that had blown off the roof had also shattered the tiles so that our slightest movement resulted in a lot of clinking and crackling sounds. On a silent night, these sounds would be a dead giveaway. Fortunately, this was not a silent night. The shouts of, "Hurry up! Hurry up!" were heard all the way up to the tower from downstairs in the courtyard. A lot of shuffling, marching, commands to "Fall in!" and "Start marching!" and much more commotion gave us the camouflage needed to settle in a small area, clear it from broken tiles, take inventory of the little food we had, and figure out how many days we could survive on it. The troops were marched out, platoon after platoon. Gradually it got quiet after the brigade had gone; however, a few soldiers and their guard dogs were left behind to capture the stragglers. I hoped to God those dogs couldn't sniff as high as the tower. A few stars could still be seen in the cold pre-dawn sky.

The cold was a problem that only got worse as wet snowflakes started to fall down on us. The few days we spent on the rooftop were uneventful. All day long the military cadre that was left behind searched the building and surrounding area for stragglers. Lou and I took care to stay low, never standing up so as not to be visible from the ground. We also moved with extreme care to keep the broken tiles from making any noise. Our supply of food, mainly the lard and preserves, began to get low. We realized that our hideout was only temporary and we would need to find something more permanent. In the distance, we could hear the Russian artillery, but beyond the noise, nothing much happened. When, oh when, would the Russians start rolling toward Budapest? Occasionally noise from the courtyard below reminded us to stay cautious. The soldiers would yell out for those in hiding to come join their unit.

The soldiers brought their families to the building as we started to hear the sounds of children playing. One day I heard a little boy of five or six yell, "Papa" downstairs in the courtyard. His cry gave me a renewed determination to fight to the end, to my last breath. I wanted to hear that precious word, "Papa," from a child of my own. I knew right then and there that I would never give up because I had a future and no one was going to rob me of it.

Future? What future? The time had come to call it quits for the rooftop. Staying there would mean either freezing or starving to death. Take your pick. Lou and I started to talk about how we could leave. Obviously, there remained serious danger with soldiers occupying the first floor of the building. To get down from the tower at night under cover of darkness seemed possible, but how would we get down the stairs and out to the street without being spotted? That could be very risky.

"Lou," I said, "I think I should try to go down first. That way you can listen and find out if my escape is successful."

"No, Endre," Lou replied, "There's a good chance that you will be shot by the soldiers."

"But, Lou," I argued, "I'm a single guy and you have a wife and daughter. Your life is a lot more important than mine. I'll go first and there will be no more discussion."

Lou had to agree with my reasoning. Under the midnight sky when all was quiet, we gently lowered the ladder desperately trying not to make any sound.

"Goodbye, Lou," I whispered and then step after step I lowered myself to the top, fourth floor. When my feet hit the floor tiles, I helped push the ladder back up to Lou so he would be safe again until the time [when] he decided to abandon the hiding place. I looked around in the total darkness and felt for the wall. Then slowly I moved toward the staircase. I willed myself to breathe as I stepped, stopped to listen, and then stepped again. Slowly I reached the stairs and went down the four floors. When I reached the corridor of the ground floor, I saw light shining under the cracks of several doors and heard the sounds of drinking and card playing. This was trouble. Any moment a door could open and I would be face to face with a soldier. I knew if I was detected, I would be shot on the spot. My fear was soon realized when a door opened ahead of me three rooms down on the right. A drunken soldier wobbled out only fifteen feet away from me. I squeezed myself tight against the wall. His poor night vision from leaving a brightly lit room saved me. He rushed down the corridor to a bathroom and never saw me. I stopped breathing. I figured that I had about two to three minutes to get to the other end of the corridor to the staircase before he returned. The problem remained on how to get out to the street. I would surely be detected trying to open the huge, squeaky, entrance door. If I went all the way to the basement, however, maybe I could escape through a window. Step after step, with deliberate stops to listen in between, I got down to the basement. The basement windows would lead me to the street, but I would attract a lot of attention if anyone saw me crawling out. Not wanting to take that chance, I waited a couple of hours until all street traffic had ceased. When it was totally quiet and the street [was] empty, I gently removed the basement window and pushed myself out to the street. By the time someone in the building discovered the removed window, I would be long gone.

Out on the street I had to think fast as to where I would go. I needed a place to hide until morning. By then maybe I could brainstorm about my next destination. Slowly walking down the empty street, I found a fairly deep building entranceway dark enough where I could crouch down and be out of sight until daybreak. It was getting colder, but at least it wasn't snowing. My thoughts turned to Lou as I wondered when and how he would make his escape from the tower's roof. After a slow night passed, I got up and started walking briskly toward the center of the city as if I was going to work or school, but definitely somewhere with a purpose. It was all for show. In reality, I had no idea where I was going. My mind was blank. I walked by a Catholic church and quickly tried to get in but the doors were locked. I continued on. Suddenly, I realized my walking had taken me toward my old school building. That gave me an idea. I had attended Italian school since fourth grade, and all the janitors were my friends. Could I possibly ask one of them if they would be willing to hide me? I rang the bell hoping against hope that the Italian school might be the safest place to hide in Hungary since the Italians were allies of Hitler's Third Reich. No Hungarian Nazi would dare to inspect this building, would they? After a long wait, I heard a shuffle. The oldest janitor, Johnny, came and unlocked the door.

"Endre," he said happily, "What are you doing here?"

"I was hoping to hide here in the school from the Nazis. Can you please help me?" I pleaded.

The happy expression immediately drained from his face and was replaced by fear. Shaking his head, he stated, "We cannot do it. No, we cannot. It is too dangerous and we cannot take the risk."

Seeing my look of dejection, he felt sorry for me. "I have an idea," he said. "Across the street is Number 6 Teréz Körut. Number 6 is an S.S. protected house. The Jews who live there are doing labor for the S.S. and so they are protected. Your old classmates, the Tuscháks, live in the house. Perhaps they will take you in?" With a shrug, Johnny closed and locked the door.

Love, Grandpa

SCHOOL DAYS
November 7, 2009

Dear Andrew,

When I was six years old in 1933, my family decided to send me to a foreign language school. Hungary was a small country, less than ten million people; therefore, middle-to-upper class people insisted on their children learning foreign languages. I had a German-speaking governess from the time I was born until age six, so I spoke German as well as Hungarian. My governess's name was Ellie. Although she came from Brűner, Czechoslovakia, she was of German origin. She was like a second mother to me. Saying goodbye to her when I was school age was more than painful, it was heartbreaking. Because I spoke German so well, my parents decided to enroll me in the Budapest German school. No one could know then what the future would hold.

In July 1933, Hitler suddenly became the big power in Germany. Apparently one of his first orders of business was to write me a letter of rejection to the German school because I was Jewish. At six years of age I was already unwelcome. There was not much time for selecting another school. My parents did manage to find a private school close to home where I went for first through third grade. I must have been pretty bored because I cannot remember a single memorable thing during those years of school. In fourth grade, I started at the Italian school and then the fun began. The school was great and my schoolmates became my best friends. Only once did a fellow student by the name of Horvath call me a "dirty Jew." After slamming my fist into his head, I never heard any more insults. I continued at the Italian school all the way through high school.

The Italians were very friendly toward the Jews. I never felt any prejudice nor heard an unkind word from my teachers in all my days at the Italian school. The Italian government, on the other hand, immediately complied with Hitler's demands to hand over their Jews for extermination.

Throughout all of Europe, the Jewish question was resolved easily and enthusiastically. Only one country resisted, Denmark. When the Germans insisted that all the Danish Jews be handed over to them for extermination, the Danes mobilized everything that floated from yachts, to sailboats, to freighters, to row boats, and [they] transferred their entire Jewish population through the night to neutral Sweden, beyond the Germans' reach. They did this at a great risk, yet they were determined to save as many Jewish lives as they could. In the end, less than a handful of Danish Jews died. Unfortunately for the Jews, the Danes were the minority.

The Swedes were also gutsy because, as we saw with the Germans in Hungary, the Swedes' neutrality was not guaranteed by anyone. The Germans could have marched into Sweden as retaliation. The Swedes knew this, and still they took the risk. They also issued numerous false passports to Hungarian Jews and argued with the Germans that these were

Swedish citizens.⁶ Because of the Swedes and Danes, tens of thousands of Jewish lives were saved.

Love, Grandpa

---

6 Swedish diplomat, Raoul Wallenberg, traveled to Budapest in July of 1944 and stayed until he was captured by the Russians when they liberated Hungary. During that time, he had thousands of "schutzpasses" printed and distributed to Jews which put them under Swedish protection. In this way, he saved tens of thousands of Jewish lives. Some have even estimated 100,000 Hungarian Jews were saved by Wallenberg (Kershaw 61-3).

TUSCHÁKS
November 17, 2009

Dear Andrew,

Number 6 Teréz Körut was a yellow-star "protected" house.[7] The Jews who lived there were doing manual labor for the S.S. The labor was mainly to load barges on the Danube River. The S.S. were determined to haul everything that wasn't nailed down, out and up to Austria before the Russians invaded. (Ironically, due to all the debris in the river from the bridges the Germans blew up to slow the Russian advance, those barges never moved).

Somehow, I had to get myself inside. The house offered much hope in the form of the Tuschák family. The Tuscháks and I were old friends. Their oldest daughter Zsuzsi was one year younger than I and attended the same Italian school that I did. She also had a younger sister, Kati, five years her junior. Kati was just a child, but Zsuzsi and I were friends even though we did not have any classes together. Once a week, however, we had mandatory religion classes. Everyone went to their respective religious classes, and we Jews all piled into one classroom. The rabbi who taught us was a very easy going, friendly man, so we used the religious hour mostly to work

---

[7] Jewish forced laborers resided in the "protected" house. During the day, some of the Jews loaded barges, others did clerical work for Adolf Eichmann (Hitler's "Architect" of the Final Solution) and the German S.S. at their headquarters in the hotel. Mr. Tuschák, a CPA, was an accountant for Eichmann. A German officer also lived in the house with the Jews. When the Hungarian Arrow Cross came to kill all the Jews in the house, the officer said, "If you kill them, I will kill you!" In this way, the Jews were protected until the Germans fled the Russian onslaught.

on our homework and to socialize. Zsuzsi had it all. She was absolutely gorgeous, super intelligent, spoke five languages fluently, and was very modest as well. Not only was Zsuzsi wonderful, but we boys loved to visit her, mainly because of her father. He was the greatest guy to talk to for advice and counsel. Her mama was okay, a good-hearted woman, but we couldn't open up to her like we could with Mr. Tuschák. I often thought that Mr. Tuschák would have liked to have had sons, but since he only had daughters, he treated all of us as if we were his boys. Zsuzsi and I were good friends. If we went out together, it was because she needed an escort, nothing more.

I was almost engaged already to another Zsuzsi. I had known Zsuzsi Munk since I was five or six years old. She was my great love, my partner, my best friend. All our friends knew that after the war and after college, we would marry for sure. Mr. Munk and my father were army buddies having served together in World War I. We were also neighbors in the same apartment building for ten years and the only children of our parents. (Unfortunately, Zsuzsi and her father were both killed. Her mother and I spent many hours crying on each other's shoulders until she died prematurely of a broken heart).

Love, Grandpa

MY FATHER

My father, Josef Lövinger, was born September 5, 1893, in Budapest, Hungary. The Lövinger family was upper class. My grandfather, Adolf Lövinger, made his money in ironworks, mainly fabricating bridge girders and pylons. He also owned two big apartment buildings in Budapest. The family lived in an apartment in one of them on the corner of Lövölde Ter (Marksmen Place) and Király Utca (King Street). They had servants and from what I heard, my grandmother Ida Hilf Lövinger, was a very classy lady. Unfortunately, at the age of 56, she died of cancer before I was born. She was a society lady who gave frequent parties and was much admired in the Budapest Jewish society.

When World War I broke out in 1914, my dad was 21 years old in his junior year at Pázmány Péter National Science University. My father was very good at math and an excellent draftsman, so the plan was for him to get a degree either in architecture or civil engineering and take over the ironworks business that my grandfather had built into a multinational enterprise. They were building railroad bridges as far away as Turkey. The war changed everything.

My grandfather had to buy my father a Reserve Officer's commission. The Austro-Hungarian Army during World War

I was composed of two elements; Reserve Officers and Regular Army Officers, besides the enlisted men. It was unheard of for the sons of the wealthy to be enlisted, and only professional officers of the Regular Army received a salary. This was quite costly for my grandfather. For five years, he had to finance horses, orderlies, uniforms, meals, and everything else that was needed to maintain an officer's lifestyle. The only things the government supplied were ammunition and weapons. The cost of being a Reserve Officer was high even in a short war. In a five-year war, it was staggering.

My father fought with the Germans on the Russian Front for three years, then on the Italian Front for two more. As a Ranger (Special Forces), he was always on the front line and sometimes operated behind enemy lines.

My father returned from the war at age twenty-six, a very sick man with bleeding ulcers. The stomach ulcers were a serious matter for my father. For as long as I can remember, he was very careful with his diet making sure never to eat any spices (so we all ate spice-free meals). Despite his remarkable discipline, every year or so the ulcers started to bleed. Then the doctor would put him on bed rest and he would eat only ice cream for days. This way he managed to avoid an operation and the danger of a perforated ulcer.

My father blamed the war for his baldness as well. He claimed that the constant wearing of his helmet for five years cut off the oxygen supply to his scalp, making him bald at an early age.

Years of being on the front lines and behind enemy lines

had taken a heavy psychological toll also. Too many killings, savage bayonet attacks (WWI's favored weapon), comrades dying in his arms, notifying families of their loved one's death, along with the constant fear of being killed had changed him. My father told me that he tried, but he just couldn't get himself back into a normal, pre-war lifestyle. Today's military knows more about shell shock, or post-traumatic stress, but in those days, no one paid any attention to such disorders. He was definitely not prepared to take up where he had left off five years earlier.

This created quite a lot of conflict with my grandfather. My father was the only child, the only son, the logical inheritor of the family enterprise, and he showed no interest whatsoever in finishing his education and taking over the helm. My grandfather considered him to be a lazy bum and was quite vocal about it.

My grandmother understood. She felt my father's pain. She tried to explain it to her husband, but she passed away too soon. My father and his dad never understood each other without my grandmother there to try to bridge the gap. Their relationship was like a third world war. I saw them together very little, and they were not happy times. It could have been because of my grandfather's lingering, painful illness. It is hard to be happy when one is not well. My grandfather died when I was five or six after a long bout with prostate cancer. After my grandfather died, our wealth also left us, mostly due to my father's love of horses.

When I was born in 1927, my father was still living

an upper-class lifestyle. The rental incomes from the two apartment buildings provided the luxuries of a limousine, chauffeur, servants, governess, travel abroad, and a stable of losing racehorses. Those racehorses consumed a lot of hay but never brought home the bacon.

I remember an elegant early childhood. I had plenty of toys, and I traveled to many beautiful places in Europe with my parents and governess. We went to Italy, the French Riviera, Monte Carlo, and Switzerland. I spent summers in Czechoslovakia, in the Tatra Mountains, where the air was clean and cool. The waterfalls would lull me to sleep at night, and we hiked, swam, and played all day long.

Eventually, the inheritance money ran out and the apartment buildings were sold. We moved to a one-room apartment with a communal bathroom across the courtyard that was freezing to get to in the winter. I was so embarrassed by my new circumstances that I stopped inviting friends over. I went from a pampered little prince to a pauper in just a few years. My father, on the other hand, had no problem getting used to poverty. He was flexible. He never complained, nor did he wish to work to improve our meager existence. When other people went off to their jobs, my father would go to the Savoy Coffee House to read the newspapers or play cards. Occasionally, he made a little money. One of his army buddies, Goldberg, was a textile manufacturer. Every so often he allowed my dad to sell his surplus or reject materials, enabling my dad to earn a modest commission. Then we would eat well for a while. We would even have sardine sandwiches, a great delicacy in Hungary. Otherwise we mostly ate noodles sprinkled with poppy seeds or walnuts.

My Uncle Béla provided a safety net up until his departure for America in 1941. He bought all my clothes, paid for my private tuition at the Italian School, and helped us out when we were in trouble with the rent money, which was quite often.

It's hard to believe, but in spite of all my father's physical and mental illness, my dad had a great sense of humor. Nobody could laugh louder or more heartily at a good joke or a funny story than my father. You could hear his loud and sincere laugh from blocks away. He had lots of friends and no shortage of very funny jokes. My father was an extremely popular man. There was something in his personality that commanded and received respect. He didn't expect it or demand it, but anyone who addressed him instantly took off his hat. Maybe having to make life and death decisions during the long war shaped his personality. He never ever looked down at anybody. He gave respect and he earned respect as a result.

As far as I was concerned, I got a military education in a civilian home. There was no back talking to my father. His word was the law. I do not remember ever being slapped or whipped by my father, but there were numerous times when I was ordered to kneel with bare knees on dry, hard lentils or peas. That hurt plenty. There was a favored spot in the living room, right next to the tall ceramic oven, where I spent many afternoons kneeling. It helped shape my character.

As I grew older, my father and I grew closer. I could even say that he and I became good friends. He spent much more time with me, giving me lots of advice about how to become a gentleman. Honor, Loyalty, Friendship, and Unselfishness were admired qualities that he operated under. Later, all his honesty contributed to his and my mother's demise. My father would not hear of acquiring false documents in order to save his family as some were doing. This wouldn't be honest and he would rather die. I took a different view. Staying honest when a bunch of cut throat gangsters were trying to murder you didn't make any sense to me. "Leveling the playing field" seemed to me more rational.

My father was glad to see me develop an interest in girls. He was especially pleased when I started to date the daughter of his close army buddy. Zsuzsi Munk became a good friend, a kissing friend, and a potential future bride.

My father got a big kick one Sunday afternoon when Zsuzsi and I spent half an hour kissing on a bench on the shore of Margitsziget Island. The Danube River was between us and the Buda shore. My father happened to be in Buda and his eagle eyes spotted us. I never heard the end of it.

My father was an early bird. He would wake around five in the morning and chase me out of bed. In these early hours, we would walk to the Szécsényi Public Bath House. There we would sweat in the sauna, get a rib-cracking massage, and swim laps in the swimming pool before I would leave for school. Those were precious moments together where we became buddies.

Due to my father's architectural training, he was a wiz at math. His help got me very good grades as he could explain complicated math problems in minutes.

I was very proud of my father. He had achieved a stellar military record having served as a First Lieutenant in the Austro-Hungarian Army during World War I. First Lieutenant was as high as a Reserve officer could be promoted. Only one officer, Captain Bienstock, made higher rank and was the most decorated officer. My father was told that he was the second most decorated.

War hero status gave my father a false sense of security. My father believed that he was a loyal Hungarian (he did not think of himself as a Jew)[8] and that he had earned, through five years of fighting for his homeland, the rights and privileges of a Hungarian.

On October 29, 1944, the Nazis came to our apartment building at Eötvös Utca 35 and took my father, mother, and my mother's cousin, Aunt Sándorné to Akademia Place which was a central "collection" station for Jews. From there, they were marched down Andrassy Boulevard toward the Danube River. They crossed the river and began their march toward Austria. Because of the lack of railroad support, the Nazis marched them from Budapest to Hidegség Concentration Camp on the Austrian border in a "death march" of more than one hundred miles.[9] These were the people for whom my father had fought and suffered.

The women, in high heels, tripped and fell, and if they

---

[8] Josef Lövinger's father completely financed the construction of a new synagogue. When Josef was asked to pay for his seat (a form of tithe), he became so insulted that as soon as Endre had his Bar Mitzvah, the family stopped attending services. They celebrated Jewish holidays with the relative of Endre's mother as he was growing up.

[9] (ArchiveAuthor, "'Death March' of 50,000 Hungarian Jews described at Eichmann Trial")

could not get up, they were immediately shot. The men were somewhat better off shoe wise, but they were of various ages, and in various stages of health, so they too were shot if they were too weak to get keep up.

The weather was against them. The November days were cold and rainy with a mix of snow. In street clothes, they all got wet and cold. With the lack of food, and long days of marching, they became weaker and weaker as the days and weeks wore on.

My father died in Hidegség, on Christmas Day, December 25, 1944, of a bleeding ulcer, a disability he had brought home with him from the previous war. My mother cradled his head in her lap as he vomited blood; she looked on as my father's life slowly and painfully ebbed away. My father was fifty-one years old.

THE WAIT
December 4, 2009

Dear Andrew,

Why the Russians sat sixty kilometers from Budapest for months was a mystery. Was their motivation "tit for tat" trying to get even with the Allies? The Allies had delayed the invasion until June 1944, despite the Russians begging for years for them to get moving so as to relieve pressure on the Eastern Front (Russian). The Allies were reluctant to move, however, until they concentrated an overwhelming armada on the coast of England. They vividly remembered the nearly disastrous escape of 350,000 British from Dunkirk, France, when the Germans almost succeeded in capturing the entire British expeditionary force in 1941. Under no circumstances did the British want a repeat of that calamity. This meant the Russians waited and let the allied invasion forces battle the German Army. The Russians did, however, make some effort toward Poland on the Northern Front.

There is an additional theory worth noting. Maybe the Russians ran out of ammunition and supplies. Rail connections between Russia and the west (Europe) were ancient and inadequate. Narrow-gage tracks could carry small lightweight cargo. Single tracks allowed only one-way traffic. Rail terminals in the east were choked because retrieving rolling stock from the west took too much time, so the Russians were literally frozen at their starting terminals. They depended more on truck carriers than rail carriers, which slowed their movement tragically. The [European] roads were not autobahns, but unpaved, narrow, horse and buggy carrying roads.

The lesson to remember is that good supply routes are crucial for going into battle. Eisenhower remembered this in 1952. As President he insisted on the Federal Highway Program (Interstate System) from east to west and from north to south, to make sure that, in case of war, we could transfer troops and supplies quickly to the theater where they would be needed. The Germans knew the same twenty years earlier when they built the autobahn system. The Russians, however, were way behind in transportation and we were dying as a result. The four-month delay caused the killing of 600,000 Hungarian Jews.

Love, Grandpa

LIBERATION
December 15, 2009

Dear Andrew,

I hid in the shadows observing Number 6 Teréz Boulevard and the S.S. headquarters directly across the street at the Royal Hotel. Finally, I saw my chance when the Jewish labor brigade returned home under heavy guard to Number 6. I slipped into their ranks without being noticed and upon gaining entry, immediately ran up to the Tuschák's third floor apartment. Mrs. Tuschák burst into tears when she saw me at her door.

"I have nowhere to hide," I explained, "Can I stay here with you?"

Mrs. Tuschák's reply warmed my heart, "Absolutely, Endre. You may stay as long as it takes. We will live or die together."

For the rest of November [and] into January the routine was to leave from Number 6 Teréz Körut (Boulevard) with the labor brigade in the morning, spend the day under the Nazis' watchful eyes, load the barges on the Danube River, and return in the evening. Occasionally, it was possible to slip food into my pockets like sugar or cereal without being seen. I knew it was risky because I would be shot if caught, but hunger was a great motivator. Mrs. Tuschák would have our only meal of the day waiting for us when we came home. She made beans in salt water and gave each of us just one cupful. Our little group numbered six. There were Mr. and Mrs. Tuschák, their daughters, Zsuzsi, and Kati, their eighteen-year-old cousin,

Pali Samuel, and myself. Mrs. Tuschák could have easily given her daughters more and the rest of us less, and we would not have blamed her. But she didn't. Each of us received equal portions from the very generous woman.

As a change in routine, Pali and I, along with a few other Jews, were ordered to decorate the S.S.'s thirty-foot Christmas tree in the Royal Hotel. We had to climb up high ladders, placing the ornaments just so. One time when the trimmings ran out, Pali and I were told to go to the basement and get more from storage. By this time, we could hear that the Russians were on the move by the closeness of artillery shelling. Conscious of the fact that the S.S. were within days of doing something to us Jews, I immediately looked around the basement for a potential place to hide. By one wall, there was a two-foot diameter sewer pipe. I climbed it and found a small ledge in the wall near the ceiling.

"Pali," I said, "We can use this as a hiding place in the future."

~ ~ ~

"The Russians are coming! The Russians are coming!" That was the cry of the S.S. which turned the headquarters in the Royal Hotel into chaos, if not near panic. Their dilemma was twofold: escape to avoid capture and certain death, or take everything with them that would be of value in Germany.

The pressure to take everything with them fell upon our scrawny, half-starved shoulders. There was constant shouting to hurry up and load the barges faster. When exhausted workers appeared to move too slowly to please the masters, they were beaten severely.

Russian artillery became more audible, but still there was no sign of a battle coming closer. We assumed that the liberation was just around the corner. The big challenge was to survive the next few days, or the next few weeks. But how?

Pali and I would sneak down to the basement whenever there was an opportunity to inspect our future hiding place behind the sewer pipe. The place looked good for the short term, but not for any longer period. Food and bathroom were going to be the two big problems. We estimated that we could last two or three days at the most. But that could be enough to save our lives.

The S.S. were moving out. Pali and I headed down to the basement amid the commotion while armed guards rounded the others [Jews] up and put them on trucks. As the S.S. searched the building and basement for hideaways, we hid quietly, hardly daring to breathe. Fortunately, our corner of the basement was too dark for the S.S. searchlights to spy us. We stayed in hiding on that ledge for the next three days. When the hotel was quiet and empty, Pali and I came out of hiding and hurried across the street to the Tuscháks, who miraculously had been left behind. By that time, the Russians were bombing heavily and everyone in Budapest was living in their basements.

The street fighting was intense. The Russians fought house-to-house battles with the entrenched Germans, liberating one house at a time. The greatest casualties besides the Germans (the Russians took no prisoners) were horses. There must have been thousands. People would risk their lives between bombs and bullets to go out with knives and pots and pans to cut up the dead horses and cook them. It had been a very long time since anyone had eaten meat.

The day finally came as we sat huddled in the basement when a Russian soldier called out to us, "Open the door! You are free!" Finally, the Russians and liberation had come.

Love, Grandpa

WILLIE, JOHNNIE, STEVIE

Growing up as an only child, I often begged my parents for a brother or sister, but to no avail. I didn't feel deprived because I had three boy cousins (my mother and their mother were first cousins), and I loved them as if they were my brothers.

The Rochlitz cousins were Willie, who was one year older than I; Johnnie, who was my age; and Stevie, who was one year my junior. Willie and Johnnie were big, muscular boys, but Stevie was a slow and sickly child. He spent more time in the hospital than at home.

One would expect that the two big boys would be gentle and protective of their weaker brother, but it was just the opposite. They frequently ganged up on him, and Stevie would get the short end of it. I was Stevie's only protector. Whenever I visited the boys, and they would get into it, I would jump into the fray, getting several bruises, scrapes, and an occasional black eye. No wonder Stevie kept asking for me to visit. He only felt safe when I was with them.

Visiting in Budapest in the 1930s and 1940s was easy for a child. From a very early age, I could get around without fear. All I had to do was to take the Number 6 streetcar from my apartment to theirs. It was maybe a half hour ride, but nobody paid any attention because it was commonplace for kids to travel alone. When I grew older and got my bicycle, I rode to my cousins' and spent the day with them. We would go to a nearby park and play soccer, hide and seek, and have a picnic.

My Uncle Márton Rochlitz, a pharmacist, was an orthodox Jew and observed all the Jewish holidays with full ritual. Since neither my father nor my mother were religious, we were always invited to the Rochlitz's for holiday celebrations. When we boys were still little, we weren't required to sit up at the table with the adults. Instead, we played under the big dining room table. But after we had our Bar Mitzvah, we were supposed to partake in the ceremony, and those meals became long and boring.

My cousins and I frequently went on outings together. They had a big limousine and a driver who would take us to the park, the Budapest Zoo, or to the pool.

One memorable outing was to the Comedy Theater for a Sunday afternoon children's show. The Comedy Theater was a cultural paradise in Budapest. They presented all the classics from Shakespeare to George Bernard Shaw, from Ibsen to Thornton Wilder, etc. But on Saturday and Sunday afternoons, they performed children's plays.

I must have been five or six when our two families drove to the Comedy Theater to see the German fairy tale, "Hansel and Gretel." We had the best seats: first balcony, front row. We could see all the audience, and they could see all eight of us as we filed into the first row. My cousins and I fidgeted while we waited with suspense for the show to begin. Finally, the curtain opened and the play started. After the first act, we all went down to the main lobby for juice and cookies. At the end of intermission, the bell rang and we went back to our seats. The lights went off, and the audience became quiet as we waited for the second act to begin. In the pitch dark, we waited and waited. Something must have gone wrong, we thought. Maybe an actor got sick? Finally, after five long minutes of darkness, a spotlight illuminated the left side of the stage. A very tall witch, completely dressed in black, appeared at the corner of the stage with a long switch in her hand. In a crackling voice, she started,

"Good afternoon, boys and girls. You all know if you were good or bad this past year. If you were bad, I will come take you with me."

To this, my cousin Johnnie jumped from his seat. With his arms outstretched for emphasis, he shouted as loud as he could, "I'm not going with you! You can't take me! I'm going home with my mommy and daddy!"

With that he sat down, and the theater was as quiet as a tomb for about ten seconds. Then, as if it had exploded, people started to laugh. They turned to each other saying, "That kid knows he was bad, but he won't go with the witch. He said so loud and clear."

The next day the newspapers carried the headline, "Johnnie Told the Witch He Would Not Go with Her. No Sir, He Is Going Home with His Mommy and Daddy!"

My cousin was the most famous person in Budapest for a day, all because he would not go with the witch.

Unfortunately, that was only true for the next twelve years.

In 1944, when the German Nazis [the evil witch] occupied Hungary, the deportation to death camps started immediately; first the countryside,[10] and later from Budapest. My Uncle Márton Rochlitz and his sons Johnnie and Stevie were taken to Auschwitz where they perished in the gas chamber. Willie was taken to a military labor camp, where he was executed along with some 2,000 other eighteen and nineteen year olds, to prevent the Russian Army from liberating the youngsters.[11]

Their mother, my Aunt Olga, was miraculously saved by their maid. She took my aunt to hide in the country while the Germans were collecting Jews for transport. Although Aunt Olga survived the Holocaust, the loss of her three sons and husband made her crazy with grief. She locked herself in her bedroom and would not come out or speak to anyone. She just wanted to die. When I came to say goodbye before heading west to America, she recognized me, hugged and kissed me, and gave me her family's silver, ceremonial Elijah's Cup which had been a part of our Passover celebrations together. Heartbroken and without the will to live, Aunt Olga died soon after my visit.

---

10 "Each day that June [1944] an estimated twelve thousand Hungarian Jews [from the countryside] were being killed in Auschwitz, five hundred each hour, an average of thirty a minute, one every two seconds" (Kershaw 55).

11 Willie Rochlitz, who was executed by the Hungarian Army, was first buried in a mass grave in the woods. After the war, all the bodies were exhumed and brought to Budapest where they were re-interned in the Central Jewish Cemetery. A memorial lists every one of the 2,000 plus "boys" who became martyrs. Cousin Willie's name is on the list.

THE SUITCASE
January 10, 2010

Dear Andrew,

"Hey, Nyemecki, Igyi Szuda!" (Hey, German, come here) yelled the Russian soldier from the middle of the empty street where he planted himself with his submachine gun pointed toward the windows of the apartment buildings. Absolutely fearless, he invited rifle fire upon himself, so that he could return a machine gun burst, and kill whoever took aim on him. There were not many Germans left, but the few who remained had to be eliminated by one means or another. What kind of urban warfare was this? I never saw anything like it, but if you had no fear, it was effective.

To us, the Russians were a wonder! Consider this: Russia extends over eleven time zones (the U.S. over four). The eleven time zones cover a vast area, from Europe far into Asia. Therefore, the Russian population reflected a diversity that Europeans with their small countries and homogeneous populations couldn't understand. Under the command of Marshal Voroshilov, the Russian Army looked Chinese to us although they were from Mongolia. Completely savage and primitive, they would easily kill you for your wristwatch if you hesitated after they pointed that they wanted it. No woman was safe. They would rape any female with no regards to looks or age. Looting by Hungarian citizens was permitted for the first forty-eight hours after liberation, then they would shoot you on sight if caught breaking or entering.

Their soldiers were desperately looking for food, but didn't find any. Food was long gone. Then they turned [looted] to anything that could be hauled home, or, if it was too big, they smashed it and left it in pieces. The destructive power of simple people was staggering.

At the height of the looting, I entered the famous Corvin Department Store. While hordes of people carried armfuls of merchandise down the forty-foot wide main staircase, a little old cleaning lady, with broom in hand, tearfully swept the broad stairs, just as if it was any normal working day for her. She did not take a single thing, but continued to perform her task of keeping the store neat in spite of the hundreds of people bent on destroying it.

The Russians were the supreme rulers, and every soldier had life or death decision-making power over the civilian population. For this reason, they were extremely dangerous and ruthless. Shortly after liberation, I ran into a life or death situation with a Russian soldier. The outcome was tragic for me even though I stayed alive.

When things had calmed down and life became somewhat normal in the city, I decided to go back to my old apartment and retrieve my most important family treasures, our family photos. My trip to the apartment was uneventful. The streets were calm, traffic was light. It took only fifteen minutes. The family that opened the door to my knocking was not mine. Apparently, the Hungarian government had allocated our vacant apartment to a Polish refugee family. As it turned out, the family of four blue-eyed blonds, were Polish Jews with false identity papers. I collected all the pictures and was looking for a bag or some box to carry them in. Unfortunately, I chose an alligator skin little suitcase. I was happily walking back toward Teréz Körut when a Russian soldier put his bayonet on my back. I turned around in shock as he pointed toward my suitcase.

"No, No!" I yelled. "Photos, photos," but he could care less.

He just wanted that alligator skin suitcase. One hand grabbed the suitcase, the other cocked his rifle. I had a choice to make. I started to cry. I had no idea if I would ever see my mother or father again. Now I was going to lose all my pictures of them. What could I do? By this time, the Russian had taken off with my suitcase. My memories, my childhood, were gone. I was alive!

Love, Grandpa

MY MOTHER

My mother, Erna Rosenthal, was born July 27, 1899, in Mohács, Hungary. A more tragic life is hard to imagine. From beginning to end, my mother was chosen to suffer.

Her world collapsed when she was nine years old. Her mother, Fanny Bock, walked away from her marriage to Nándor Rosenthal because she had fallen in love with the local high school teacher, Gyula Darvas. The tragedy was compounded by the fact that the family was split in two. Custody of my mother was given to her father and later stepmother, while her six-year-old baby brother, Béla, went to live in Budapest with her mother and new stepfather.

My mother told me that for nine months she lived in Mohács, Hungary, with her father and stepmother, and she cried all the time. She couldn't wait to join her mother and little brother Béla during the three summer months.

After her father remarried, my mother's life became pure hell. Her stepmother was insanely jealous and mean. Each day in Mohács was a struggle: no girlfriends and definitely no boyfriends. Despite her uncaring stepmother, her father sent her to a finishing school in Lausanne, Switzerland. There she learned to speak perfect German and French, and she became a very fine pianist. At the finishing school, my mother also learned how to be a perfect hostess and a fantastic cook.

By age twenty-five, my mother had never dated anyone and was destined to be an old maid. Lo and behold, an old aunt, Katica néni (aunt) had a prospect for my mother. Katica néni had an apartment at Kiraly Utca 42 (42 King Street) whereas the Lövingers lived only a few blocks apart in the apartment building they owned at Kiraly Utca 1. I don't know how her mother's aunt and the Lövingers met, but Katica néni wrote to my mother in Mohács to please hurry to Budapest because she knew of a handsome, eligible bachelor. My mother took her aunt's advice and rushed to Budapest. She and her "little brother," twenty-two-year-old Béla, met the Lövinger bachelor at Katica néni's apartment.

Josef Lövinger hired a horse drawn carriage to ride out to City Park (Városliget) and to have a fancy lunch at Gundel's, an elegant restaurant in the park. This made such a big impression on brother Béla that he was all in favor of my mother marrying Lövinger. The Lövingers were an old Budapest family for hundreds of years, so Béla hoped that his beloved sister would move to Budapest permanently where they could see each other often.

My mother who was six years younger than Lövinger, was impressed with his "worldliness" and also that he was well educated and gentlemanly. He was handsome in a rugged way and had an absolutely charming personality.

My father fell hopelessly in love with my mother. He was taken in by my mother's beauty and elegance as well as her impressive piano playing. This was very important to him because my father loved to play piano. He had attended the Liszt Ferenc Music Academy while studying at Pázmány University. Together they would play a beautiful duet. They married in August 1926.

Their first apartment was in my grandfather Lövinger's building on Lövölde Ter, but by the time I was born in 1927, they had moved to their other apartment building at 81 Izabella Utca. There was a balcony where I was parked quite a lot to inhale the fresh air. We lived there for many years until my father lost all his money and the two apartment buildings he had inherited from my grandfather. I'm sure this saddened my mother, but she never made any demands on my father. She always did her best to provide wonderful meals for us, and I never heard her complain. Never.

There are not enough superlatives to describe my mother. Loving, sweet, calm, friendly, intelligent, elegant, would be just the beginning. Needless to say, I was crazy about my mother and always tried to please her.

My mother had a good sense of humor and would laugh readily, but I always detected a deep sadness in her eyes. The many years of separation from her mother and beloved brother left an indelible mark on her soul from which she never recovered.

While we suffered many years of poverty, that was nothing compared to what was in store for us after the Nazis occupied Hungary in 1944. My father and I believed we would survive the Nazi scourge, but my mother had an uncanny sixth sense and knew better. She pleaded with my father to temporarily convert to Catholicism in order to get lifesaving documents, but to no avail. The Allies and the Russians were much too slow in destroying the Nazi empire, and she knew instinctively that time would run out for the Jews.

I said goodbye to my mother for the last time on October 19, 1944, and saw the tears running down her cheeks as I was marched out of our building at Eötvös Utca 35. Ten days later, on October 29, 1944, the Nazi's began the "Clean Sweep" program to cleanse Budapest of all Jews. My mother and father, together with an estimated 50,000 Jews, were forced into a death march[12] of over one hundred miles from Budapest to Hidegség Concentration Camp[13] near the Austrian border.

My mother was devastated after my father died. I can only imagine her pain and heartache, her sorrow and tears as she watched helplessly while my father slowly suffered. She had Aunt Sándorné with her who tried to console her. But what consolation was there for her? Her husband was dead, and her son? She had no idea if I was alive or dead, and she would have been greatly worried about my ability to survive. In the previous summer, I had been diagnosed with a heart condition, an enlarged heart. Doctors put me on bed rest for a long time and gave me medication. I was still weak and very out of shape. My mother had seen during the march how the

---

[12] In the mass murder of Adolf Eichmann's "Death Marches", "Hungarian guards whipped the Jews as they staggered toward the border, some dying on their feet, most as they lay on the ground having collapsed from exposure and hypothermia…if they slowed, they were killed" (Kershaw 106-108).

[13] Typhus, exhaustion, freezing, or being shot at, were the main cause of death [at Hidegség]… "We were treated like animals…if someone couldn't keep up and sat down, they got shot," said Istavan Horvath, a survivor. Camp was closed March 28, 1945 (Levéltár, Magyar Zsidó, "Hidegség").

weak were treated, how merciless the guards were.

When the troops gathered the Jews to continue the march into Austria, my mother was very weak and could hardly drag herself. Her cousin was either equally weak, or just did not want to abandon my mother. I do not know. Mrs. Winkler, who was in Hidegség with her young daughter, Marika, told me that both my mother and Aunt Sándorné were taken to the pretty picturesque railroad station, and there they were machine-gunned to death together with all the others who didn't look like they could handle the continued march.[14] My mother was forty-five years old.

I cannot imagine how my mother managed to cover over one hundred miles in high heels. My mother only wore heels. I can see her stumbling and even falling during those cold, wet, nasty November days. Perhaps my father in his ailing condition was able to support her along the way, or perhaps she had to support him. Either way, it was an absolute miracle that she made it all the way to Hidegség.

Some people can forget, and even forgive all the atrocious, savage, and hateful behavior that characterized the Nazis. Unfortunately, I am not a good forgiver. But, if you knew my mother and my father, you would understand the scars I wear whenever I think of them. I try to closet the horrors and just remember the wonderful times we three had together.

---

14 After the war, the Hungarian Jewish Community arranged to open the mass grave at Hidegség and bring all the bodies back to the Budapest Central Jewish Cemetery. Endre found his father's name engraved on the stone. His mother's name was not listed because she did not die in camp. He never found out what happened to his mother's body, so he had her name added next to his father's.

HEARTACHE

The Russians had finally arrived and with them LIBERATION! FREEDOM! How long I had waited to hear those words! Free from being hunted by the Nazi monsters, I went to see if Lou Winkler was home. He was delighted to see me and insisted I stay with him. His wife and daughter were still missing. Lou and I spent our days scavenging for any food we could find. All of Budapest was starving. One time we brought home a fifty-pound block of chocolate not realizing until the first bite that it was unsweetened. Yuck! Its bitterness made it hard to eat but we finished it off.

Five days after liberation, Mrs. Winkler and daughter Marika arrived at the apartment from Hidegség.

Tearfully, Mrs. Winkler told me how my father died in my mother's arms on Christmas Day. Then she went on to say how my sweet, gentle mother and Aunt Sándorné Lustig were executed by Nazi machine guns. There are no words to describe my heartache.

Often things seem much nicer when one looks back, and they tend to take on a romanticized version of the facts. But in the case of my mother and father, their love for each other was so pure, so unconditional, that I will forever consider myself lucky to have grown up in such a glow of warmth and love.

Theirs was a beautiful romance producing so much love that the excess spilled over onto me.

The Winklers insisted that I remain with them in their three-room apartment. The survivor's bond made us into a special kind of family.

RUSSIANS
January 20, 2010

Dear Andrew,

The Russians turned out to be a lot more trouble as time went on. We were hoping for liberation from the Nazi monsters, instead we got occupation from the Mongolian hordes. If it was only unpleasant, we could have coped with that. But quickly, it turned into a life or death challenge.

One day, I was walking the streets in search of some food. Anything I could put in my mouth would do. I was hungry to say the least. Stores had all been emptied. People were carving up the dead horses shot in combat and frozen due to cold weather. This was their only hope for protein. There were quite a lot of dead horses lying in the street, so people were busy with knives, saws, and buckets.

I was grabbing a piece of meat, when a Russian soldier spotted me and ordered me to follow him. What did he want with me or from me? I had no idea. We were walking from one street to another, and pretty soon I saw a whole bunch of people, mostly young men, milling around, and guarded by a number of Green Caps, the Russians equivalent to the German S.S. The group kept growing and growing. By the time [I got there], I estimated two hundred of us; the Russians formed us into columns of four and started us marching toward the outskirts of Budapest. After some hours of marching, we arrived at a big square. At the end of the square was a very large school building. We were hungry, cold, and tired. The Russians opened the school doors and marched us inside where they started filling, filling, and filling the empty classrooms. They packed us in so tightly, that we could not even sit down. We were forced to stand upright shoulder to shoulder the entire night. This must have been some form of Russian crowd control, because by not being able to move, sit, or to lie down, you can't cause an awful lot of trouble. It didn't take me long to figure out that this was big trouble and that by hook or crook, I had to part company with this march to hell.

Confirmation came the next morning. Still dark, around five o'clock, they chased us out of the building and assembled us in the square. A German-speaking Russian major spoke, "You, Hungarians! (Me Hungarian? I'm a Jew. For the past four years, I was told I was not Hungarian. So, when did I become one?) You Hungarians, together with your German friends, destroyed a good deal of Mother Russia! Now, we give you the opportunity to come and help rebuild our beautiful country."

This was all I had to hear. I was getting out of there, the sooner the better. It was dark and there was a lot of milling around. The square was heavily guarded by the Russian Green Caps, but there was no spotlight and visibility was very poor. On one side of the square, I spotted a bunch of Hungarian peasant women in their big, broad skirts, standing in line, waiting before dawn for the bakery shop to open. Now was my chance. I milled around inside the crowd, gradually working my way toward the edge. When a bunch of commands created a mini riot within the crowd, I took off, practically flying toward the line of peasant women. Almost collapsing from the effort, I yelled to the women, "Hide me. Hide me please!"

They were in shock and practically paralyzed with fear, but they didn't move as I crawled under the multi layered peasant skirt of one of the women. She remained motionless. Luckily for me the bakery was thirty minutes from opening, so I waited in hiding until the unfortunate crowd was marched out of the square. When I emerged from underneath the skirt, the square was empty. I thanked the women and started my walk back toward Budapest. I don't know if the others ever returned.

Love, Grandpa

GRANDMOTHER

As the only grandchild of my dear grandmother, Mrs. Gyula Darvas, I was the "apple of her eye," until the day she died.

My grandmother, Fanny, was the fifth and youngest daughter of Erzsébet Svab and Bernát Bock, a landowner in Kácsfalu, which was part of the Austro-Hungarian Empire (later it became part of Yugoslavia, and eventually Serbia).

The Bock family was fervently hoping for a son to take over the estate, when for the fifth time they got a daughter. My great-grandfather Bernát decided to rear Fanny as a boy. She learned how to ride a horse when she was very young. She was trained to be an overseer: bossy and commanding. She told me the story of when she was out riding her horse who had just returned from military service, when a group of cavalry troops came galloping down the road. Grandmother's horse automatically took off to join up with the military detail. She furiously whipped the horse to obey her commands and ignore the troops. The soldiers were laughing their heads off when they saw the pretty young woman trying to steer her big horse away from them.

Another time her horse stopped abruptly when she was at a full gallop. She tried to nudge the horse forward not knowing why it was so hesitant. She dismounted, looked ahead, and saw a big snake crawling in the middle of the dirt road. Grandmother looked around and found a fallen tree branch. She went back and beat the snake until it finally moved out of the road. She remounted and trotted off.

Trouble started when it was time to find a husband for Fanny. She was beautiful, but not a bit feminine. Young men came, taken in by her beauty, but left quickly when they discovered her masculinity. It was time to engage the matchmaker.

The matchmaker started her search in Mohács, the closest city to Kácsfalu. There she found a merchant by the name of Nándor Rosenthal who was slightly older than Fanny. Grandpa Rosenthal was quickly smitten by the beauty of Fanny, but she was not so sure she needed to get married. Eventually she gave in and they wed in 1898, but Fanny missed the farm and her previous lifestyle terribly.

My grandmother was a young bride of twenty when she married thirty-two-year-old Nándor Rosenthal on February 4, 1898, in Siklós, Hungary. The twelve-year difference, and the fact that my grandmother was a "bossy" person weighed heavily upon the marriage. They had two children: my mother, born on July 27, 1899, and her younger brother, Béla, born on September 2, 1902. The marriage was not a happy one.

They lived in Mohács, Hungary, where my grandfather had his business. Somehow my grandmother fell in love with the local high school teacher, Gyula Darvas. One thing led to another, and sometime in 1907, she left her husband, Nándor. On January 20, 1908, she married Darvas, and they moved to Budapest. The heartbreaker was the splitting up of the children. My Uncle Béla who was only six years old went with his mother, while my mother Erna, who was just nine, went with her father.

Darvas and my grandmother had no children of their own, but Darvas turned out to be a good stepfather to my Uncle Béla and a generous stepfather to my mother when she spent summers in Budapest. As a former high school teacher, he was definitely child oriented, had a good sense of humor, and was respected in his community. He earned his living by importing and selling southern produce like prunes, nuts, raisins, figs, dates, and bananas from the tropics. When I was a Boy Scout leader, I would take my platoon to visit his warehouse once a month where he allowed us to fill our paper bags with all kinds of goodies. My popularity with my scouts increased with these visits.

After some years, relations cooled, and my step-grandfather moved out in 1931. My grandmother went on welfare. For some reason, she didn't get alimony or any financial assistance from Darvas. This was surprising because my step-grandfather had a very successful business and also earned a good salary as a "city father" (alderman). Along with support from the state, she also received financial help from her son, my very generous Uncle Béla.

Grandmother and Darvas remained good friends until she died in 1941. He would come by once a week to have lunch with Grandmother and seemed to be concerned about her health, but not enough to help her financially. When I asked my step-grandfather why he left my grandmother, he replied he was looking for tender loving care which he didn't get from my grandmother. I could have told him so, knowing my grandmother's upbringing.

My grandmother moved to very humble lodgings, a one-room apartment. Two years later, in 1934, my father went bankrupt. We were forced to move out of our big apartment at 81 Izabella Utca and move in with Grandmother until 1944.

With all the inconveniences of crowded space and an outside toilet, the advantage was living together with my grandmother whom I adored. She was smart and witty but never mushy or soft. She was a strong, commanding lady who never hesitated to bop me over the head with her cane if I misbehaved or tried to sneak her a smooch or hug.

My grandmother's chief concern was that I should not be spoiled. As an only child, it was natural for me to get a lot of attention, adult attention. She wanted me to grow up to be a man capable of making it in a bad, nasty world. For this reason, she encouraged me to become a Boy Scout so I would learn survival skills, become a skier, be more athletic, and learn to fight back whenever bad boys wanted to harm me. Scouts helped me gain self-confidence, and later when the Nazis invaded, all those different skills guided me in my various escapes.

When I was five, Grandmother and I went on a vacation together to her sister Caroline's in Siklós. Aunt Caroline was a widow whose home was situated on the market square. I would kneel in the window on market days and watch with excitement all the live animals that the peasants and gypsies brought to market: chickens, ducks, geese, horses, lambs, and pigs. I was shocked to observe how the gypsies fed their babies. The mother first chewed up the food, then scraped it from her mouth and pushed the mush into her baby's mouth. It was not at all appetizing to watch.

High above the village, on top of the tallest hill, stood an old Turkish fortress. The village children and I played war from morning until evening, re-enacting the Battle of Mohács in 1650 when the Turks overran Hungary, and [then] occupied it for 150 years.

About six miles north of Siklós, in Harkany, was one of Hungary's famous sulfur baths. Grandmother and I took an unforgettable rickety bus ride to Harkany. The space on the bus was divided between animals going to market and passengers.. The noise and bumps were unbelievable. The old bus had lost its shocks ages ago. When we got to the sulphur baths, they were good for the joints if you could stand the rotten egg smell. I wanted to escape from the smell as quickly as possible, but Grandmother luxuriated in them and always wanted to stay just a little longer. It was paradise for her.

My grandmother suffered a debilitating stroke that paralyzed her left side shortly before my family moved in. My mother took good care of her, eventually helping her regain some of her lost movement. It was a difficult task for my mother, especially in a little one-room-and-kitchen apartment with an outside toilet. My Uncle Béla helped by hiring a nurse and renting a spacious apartment in Buda for my grandmother. She was comfortable there until my uncle emigrated to America in 1941 and couldn't help anymore. My grandmother moved back in with us, but died soon after. We buried her in the Central Jewish Cemetery in Budapest.

I will never forget how heartbroken I was when she passed away. We had a short service at the cemetery synagogue, then they put her coffin on a two-wheeled pushcart. All the way from the synagogue to her gravesite we walked behind the cart and I cried. I was fourteen at the time, old enough to realize what a great champion my grandmother was. Later I would realize how wise she had been to toughen me; I needed the survival skills that would save me from the horrible death the Nazis had planned. Somehow, my grandmother foresaw that awful times were coming. My grandmother insisted on my ability to walk through fire and to fight back when odds weren't in my favor. She was a no nonsense, capable, tough old lady, with tons of love within which she would never express nor let others express to her.

NICK ROCHLITZ
January 20, 2010

Dear Andrew,

My guardian angel appeared in person one day. Starvation in Budapest became life threatening. The stores that were emptied long ago never got restocked. The horses that were killed in battle were stripped so that only bones remained. Slowly we were running out of hope. That is when a cousin by the name of Nick Rochlitz appeared, looking for our mutual Uncle Sándor Lustig. I had never met this cousin before, I hadn't even known of his existence. We weren't blood related, but related or not, he was bringing good news.

Nick had become a partisan and was fighting with the Russian forces after the liberation of Budapest. Because of this, he had almost all the privileges of a Russian soldier: documents, travel permits, etc … He said he had an apartment in the city of Debrecen (about 200 miles east of Budapest) and invited me to come and visit him, promising that Debrecen was loaded with food. Debrecen was the capital of the Hungarian plains, the breadbasket of Europe. This sounded good, but without a travel permit one couldn't board a train.

"Don't worry," he said. "I can get a copy of my travel permit, and you can use it in my name to get yourself to Debrecen before you starve to death."

Music to my ears! He was as good as his word. A couple of days later he brought me copies of all his documents. He urged me to hustle down to the train station and take the first train to Debrecen. I did exactly as he said, but when I entered the station, I was greeted with a scene of total chaos. There were hundreds of people milling around: some sitting, some sleeping on the platforms, all waiting for a train to board. There was no schedule, no timetable, no order. Trains rolled at a whim. No one could tell me when the next train would depart. I didn't know if this was a Russian strategy to keep people uninformed, or if it was a necessity, making troop movement a priority. Hungary, previously with a record of on-time departures and arrivals, was now completely disorganized. No use in fighting city hall, [so] I carved out a sitting place for myself, pulled an overcoat around me, and tried to snooze. Who knew how long the wait would be. About six or seven hours later, a slow-moving passenger train backed into the station. In a flash, everyone was on their feet, and as soon as the train stopped, hundreds of people were climbing up the train stairs, including me. Suddenly there was an arm around my waist pulling me down from the train.

"Hey, Bourgeois. Igyi szuda (come here)," said a Russian soldier as he pulled me off the train. "Where are you going?"

I was thinking, 'what business is it of yours?'

"Got documents?" he asked.

"Yes, I have documents. What do you want?" I answered.

"Come with me," he ordered.

He marched me out of the station to the square in front where we crossed the avenue, and into an apartment building which appeared to be a Russian police station. We walked up three floors, when he opened a door and pushed me inside. Once again, it was jammed packed, standing room only, shoulder to shoulder. How did I get into this lousy predicament? Why had he singled me out among the hundreds of passengers? Why does he think I'm a bourgeois, or middle class, boy when I'm dressed in rags? I dreamed of all the good food my cousin promised [that] awaited me in Debrecen: chicken, ham, cheese, chocolate cake. Here I was starving, with good food just a few hours away, being imprisoned on an empty stomach. What was my crime? Somehow, I had to figure a way to get out of this place fast!

Love, Grandpa

TRIP TO DEBRECEN
January 31, 2010

Dear Andrew,

A Russian captain was the interrogator. He spoke in German.

"Do you have documents?" he questioned.

Now, I had a serious dilemma. I actually had two sets of documents in my pockets. My own, of course, but also the partisan documents of my "cousin" Rochlitz. Which should I produce and present to the captain? Making a mistake here could cost me my life. I decided to take a chance. I gave him the partisan documents. He seemed to mellow a little when he saw that "I" had been fighting with the Russian Army for several months.

"Name?"

I gave him the Rochlitz name.

"Age?"

"Twenty-four," I answered.

He was a little surprised and looked at me with wide eyes since I was not even eighteen at the time.

"Hmmm, twenty-four?" but he did not pursue it. "Why did they bring you here?"

Here was my chance to voice a flood of complaints.

"You're asking me? Why did they bring me here? That dumb soldier practically dragged me off the train for no good reason whatsoever. All I'm trying to do is to get back to my home in Debrecen. Is that a crime? He never even asked for my documents, just grabbed me, and dragged me here. Do I look like an enemy of the Red Army? You, dear captain, can see the injustice of this all and will surely let me go because I have done nothing to deserve this kind of nasty treatment, when I'm a documented friend."

"Okay, okay," the captain said. "Don't get yourself all worked up over nothing. You can go. Stay out of trouble in the future."

Whew! I dodged one big bullet. If they had searched and found two sets of documents on me, I would be on the next train to hell; not to Debrecen but to Siberia or certain death! From now on, I would watch my back. It wouldn't matter where I was or what I was doing, I was going to have 360-degree vision. Nobody was going to sneak up on me again.

I started walking out of the building to the busy railroad station, traffic all around me, people busily rushing to and fro, as I returned to the land of the living after my hellish experience. Taking a deep breath, I purposefully walked to the station. Once there, I looked for the next train to Debrecen along with at least five hundred others.

When the train doors opened for boarding, the rush was bone crushing with the pushing and shoving; some young guys climbed to the roof of the cars, others stood on the couplings. There was not an inch of open space left. All these people were starved and had heard there was food available in the country. The train pulled slowly out of the station to destination FOOD! Thirty miles out of Budapest things started to improve. The train pulled to a stop, and peasant women alongside the track were hawking apples. Within minutes, passengers had grabbed every apple for sale and were munching on crunchy apples. The train pulled away chug-chugging toward Hatvan, sixty miles from Budapest. In Hatvan the food offered was more plentiful: hard boiled eggs, hot bread with butter, apple cider, even cookies! We thought we must be in paradise, or getting close to it. We were soon to find out that paradise was only another thirty to forty miles away. About one hundred miles from Budapest, the offering was now ROASTED CHICKENS! Chickens! I had not seen chickens in many months! This was fantastic! Would there be a chocolate cake at the end of the journey? Guess what? Yes, there was a chocolate cake in Debrecen waiting for me. What was more? There was even whipped cream on top of it. I ate with such gusto and enthusiasm that for the next week I was sick as a dog. My stomach was not used to all this rich food, so I had to "pay the piper."

Love, Grandpa

My mother Erna Rosenthal
Lövinger at age 18

Grandmother Fanny Bock
(Rosenthal) Darvas

Uncle Béla Rosenthal (Ross)

Aunt Sophie Rosenthal (Ross)

*I took this picture of my mother and father
sitting by the Danube River around 1941*

My father Josef Lövinger

*Father and Aunt
Sophie playing cards*

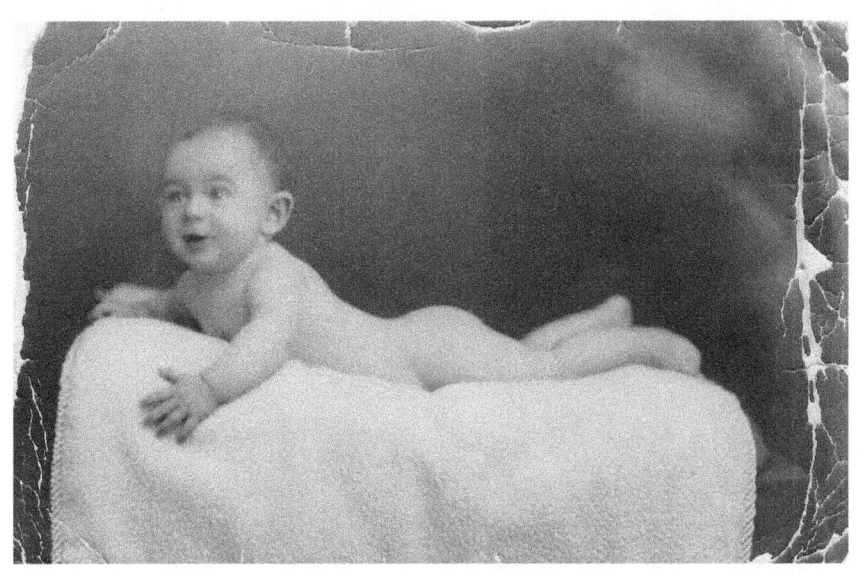

My baby picture 1927

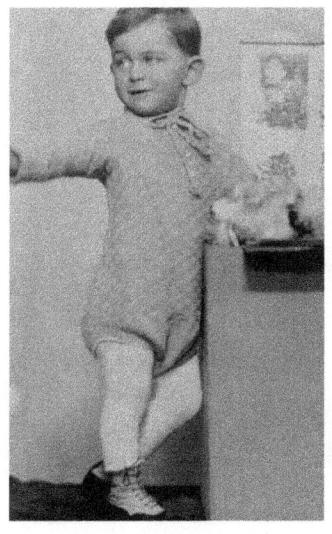

Me as a toddler

With my mother when I was 8

Me with my mother

*My father took this picture of me with
my mother by the Danube River*

*Picnic at Városliget (City Park), Budapest 1940-1941
From left-My father, Sass, a fellow Boy Scout, Zsuzsi's
uncle, my mother, Zsuzsi's aunt, me, Zsuzsi Munk,
Zsuzsi's aunt, Zsuzsi' mother, Zsuzsi's father. The only
survivors were Zsuzsi's mom, one aunt, and me.*

At 8 years of age

*Best Man at Nick and
Rose Rochlitz's wedding*

Mr. Schulzer

Lou Winkler saying Kaddish at my father's mass grave

*My daughter, Deborah Erna Oury,
with Mrs. Winkler in Budapest*

*Deborah Erna at my
grandmother's grave*

Deborah Erna with Mrs. Tuschák in Haifa, Israel

In my law school days.

Vice President Mid-Western Sales for Kurt Orban Company, 1971

With my grandson Andrew the day he graduated fron the Air Force Academy

With my lovely bride, Judy Crane Ross

My bedroom was the first window to the left of the balcony

Sitting on the bench at Margitszget Island where I got my very first kiss from Zsuzsi Munk

In front of my apartment in the courtyard of the Yellow Star house at 35 Eötvös Utca

Where my parents last saw me at age 17 before I was marched out of the courtyard

Nyugati Train Station in Budapest where the Russians captured me as I was catching the train to Debrecen in search of food, and where Mr. Polgár worked

Visiting my father's mass grave among the victims of Hidegseg, Auschwitz, etc

View of the Danube River and the destruction of Budapest in the Spring of 1945.

Elisabeth Bridge where I made my first escape.

Marika Winkler, Budapest, Hungary

The note my parents sent to me at Labor Camp, addressed to...Lowinger Endre and Lusztig Sandor, Opposite of Soroksar ice factory, in the chemistry factory. On the Erzebet-kecskemet Highway, 73-111unit

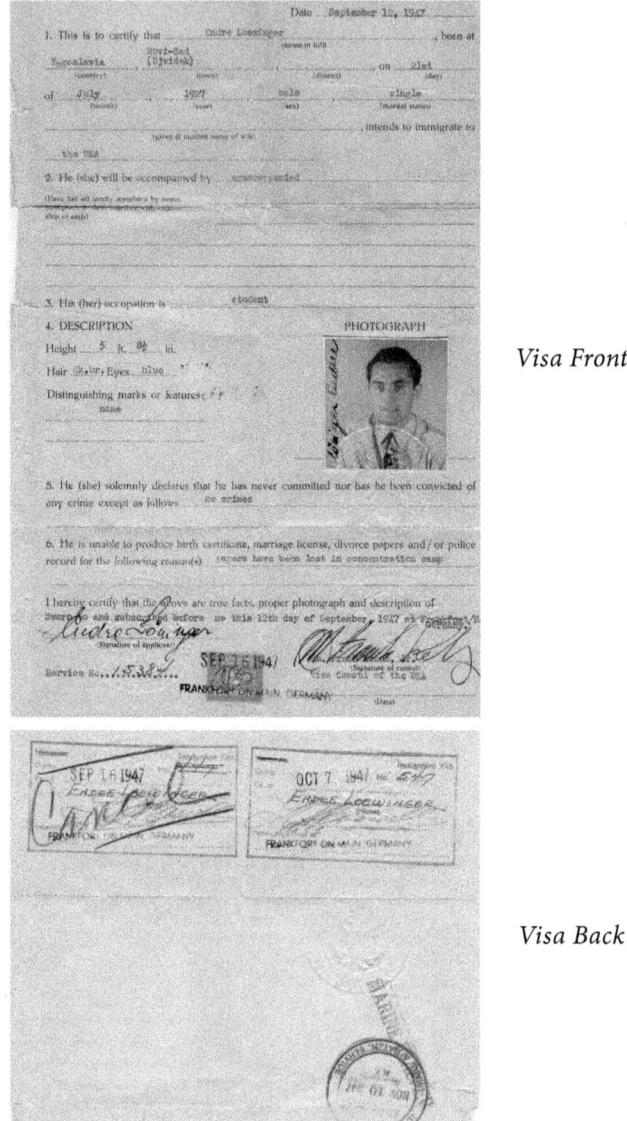

Visa Front

Visa Back

Ross Family photo 1962
From L to R, Peter, Deborah, Judy, me, Jamie, Matthew

Ross Family photo 2015
Back Row: John, Deborah, Peter, Matthew
Front Row: Judy and me

Army Buddies in Germany 1955- Fred Smith, Philip Crane (future brother-in-law) and me.

PART 2: DESTINATION AMERICA

COLONEL TEDDY EHRENTHÁL
February 10, 2010

Dear Andrew,

Life at the Winklers' [after my trip to Debrecen] was relatively quiet and consisted of looking for food and heating fuel. One day, however, there was a big commotion in our courtyard. A bunch of Russian soldiers led by a high-ranking colonel were rushing from apartment to apartment looking for someone.

"Lövinger, Lövinger. Where is my friend, Lövinger?" hollered the colonel.

I stepped up to him and said, "Colonel, I'm sorry to say my father, Josef Lövinger, and my mother, Erna Lövinger, are both dead. I am the only Lövinger who survived."

He rushed to me, hugged me, kissed me, and started to cry. It turned out that Colonel Teddy Ehrenthál was a close army buddy of my father's when they both served as second lieutenants during World War I in the Austro-Hungarian Army on the Russian front. Apparently, my father had saved the colonel's life; however, my father couldn't save him from later becoming a prisoner of the Russians. He was put in a Russian prisoner-of-war camp where he survived. When the communists took over, he promptly escaped and rushed to Paris, France. In France, he got into the theater business and eventually became president of the Societé de Gaumond, Europe's most famous theater chain. When the Nazis started World War II in 1938, he predicted major trouble for Jews.

He returned to Russia, joined the army, became a colonel, and because of his language skills, he was assigned to the staff of Marshal Voroshilov, Commander of the Soviet Southern Theater.

Now in Budapest, he was searching for my family. When he found out that my mother and father had perished, he wanted to take care of me to repay my father's bravery in saving him. Therefore, he asked me to pack my belongings because I was to move into his spacious apartment where he lived with his girlfriend.

I was a bit hesitant. I still didn't trust the Russians since my harrowing experience shortly after occupation, but the colonel assured me that I would be safe and that I would never be hungry again.

Reluctantly, I packed my few things, got into his staff car, and drove a quarter mile to his apartment which was on Körönd, one of the major squares in Budapest. The apartment was just one floor above the Savoy Coffeehouse, where my dear father spent most of his short, tragic life, sipping coffee, and reading all the newspapers and magazines.

The colonel's apartment was big. I met his girlfriend, a Hungarian lady, not too pretty and not too bright. As it turned out, it was my job to babysit her while the colonel was at work.

There was plenty of food just as the colonel promised, and in Budapest at that time, that was nothing to sneeze at. I proceeded to fatten myself up.

The days were routine; however, one day the colonel came home very excited. Marshal Voroshilov was giving a reception and we were invited. I must confess, I was not too thrilled since I didn't speak one word of Russian. But the colonel wanted to show me off as a holocaust survivor, and there was no way out. The colonel bought me clothes so I could change out of my rags and be presentable to the High Command.

I met Voroshilov. I met his staff. But the most wonderful meeting was with Russian caviar! It was a sight I had never seen before. Sturgeon caviar was pressed into big blocks like cheese. With a small knife, you could scrape slices off the block and smear them on little pieces of bread. I parked myself next to the biggest block of caviar I had ever seen and gorged until I was so full I couldn't eat one more bite.

Instead of drinking champagne with the caviar, the Russians drank vodka. Pretty soon they were singing, dancing, and becoming loud and boisterous. They were having as much fun as possible before proceeding the next day to go and kill Germans. There was something naïve and childish when I observed them. I did not know if that was because of their nature, or if war made people like that.

One evening when the colonel returned home, he announced he had been given orders to move west.

"Colonel," I said, "I don't want to appear ungrateful. You've given me shelter and very good meals, but I have to think of my future. It is time for us to part company."

"What do you want to do?" he asked.

"I want to attend the University to become a lawyer," I replied.

"Well, if that is what you want, I can't stop you. I will miss you and so will my girlfriend."

"Thank you, Colonel," I said. "I'll leave tomorrow."

The next day I moved out and never saw the colonel again.

I do not think the colonel had a happy ending. The problem was Comrade Stalin. After the war was over, the two Marshals, Voroshilov (Southern Army) and Zhukov (Northern Army), were made Heroes of the Soviet Army. They got a lot of admiration, parades, receptions, and decorations. Sooner or later this attention became a source of great displeasure for Stalin.

"Zhukov," Stalin said. "You are trying to steal the limelight from me! Remember, I won the war against the Germans, not you! For your insubordination, you are exiled to your dacha (summer home) until I say so. Go and get out of here."

"Voroshilov," said Stalin. "You're a headline grabber! The newspapers are full of what you did in Odessa and Leningrad. They keep forgetting what I did for Russia! Go to your dacha and stay until I forgive you."

So, the two biggest war heroes were deprived of their well-earned hero worship and disappeared from the scene. Rumor had it that their able staffs were deported to Siberia and made to work in the mercury mines, where they perished.

The Battle of Stalingrad was one of the most dramatic reversals of fortune in the history of warfare. It decimated the German Army so it could never regroup and threaten Russia again.

Love, Grandpa

UNIVERSITY
February 21, 2010

Dear Andrew,

After saying goodbye to Colonel Ehrenthál, his girlfriend, and the elegant apartment, I packed my little bag and moved back in with the Winklers, but not for long.

One nice warm spring day, a life-long friend of my Uncle Béla arrived to move me in with his family upon my uncle's request. The gentleman was Joseph Schulzer, who before the war, was the executive vice president of all Hungarian coal mines. His wife, Bertha, and their daughter Magda, had all survived. They lived in a beautiful fourth-floor apartment, encompassed by a terrace, only one block from the Parliament Building.

I packed my bag, said goodbye to the Winklers, and moved into luxury once again with the Schulzers. My life was settling down. The main goal was still to get myself to America to join my uncle and aunt as soon as possible. The second goal, while I was waiting to emigrate, was to do something useful with my life. I enrolled to study law at the National University, Pázmány Péter.

In Hungary, like all over Europe, liberal arts education was nonexistent. After you finished high school, you entered professional school, usually a six-year course. After six years, you would have your Phd., M.D., or J.D., in medicine, law, architecture, chemistry, etc. This is why every other person is doctor this or doctor that in Europe.

So, I started at the University, and guess what? By this time Hungary was a totally communist country. However, I found myself studying Canon Law, or law of the Catholic Church in Latin (typical in Europe, except in England, where they taught British Common Law).

"HANC EGO REM EX IURE QUIRITIUM MEAM ESSE AIO"

I had to learn the entire judicial proceeding, word by word, in Latin! Right away I was sorry I chose law. I should have chosen economics which I liked better anyway. But I kept trudging along, memorizing page after page, eventually finishing freshman year.

Foremost in my thoughts was getting to America. But that was a lot harder than I imagined. Why? Because of emigration quotas that had not been loosened after the war. Hungary had a microscopic quota of only a few hundred a year. At that rate, I could be waiting ten years, for heaven's sake! Luckily, I had an escape. Officially I was Hungarian, but I was born in the city of Novi Sad, which had once been part of the Austro-Hungarian government. Now it was part of Yugoslavia, and I could claim Yugoslav citizenship which had a much higher quota.

Life at the Schulzers was very pleasant. I had fallen in love with their maid, Margaret. She was eight years older than I and beautiful. She was also beautiful inwardly. She was the reason the Schulzers were alive. She had hidden all three Schulzers for over six months at the risk of her own life should she be found out. She had hidden them in two beds where she covered them with large down comforters. They stayed that way the entire day. Only at night, in complete darkness, were they able to clean themselves, eat, and go to the bathroom. The strain and stress was so great that Mr. Schulzer died of a heart attack shortly after I arrived in America. But Margaret was some special hero: unselfish, devoted, fearless, and also loving and caring.

Love, Grandpa

PACKAGES FROM AMERICA
March 2, 2010

Dear Andrew,

The war in Europe was over in 1945, and Jewish relatives in America were desperately trying to find out what had become of their loved ones. For the first time, American newspapers revealed the horrors of the German Final Solution. Americans were made aware of the death camps and the unbelievable cruelty of the Nazis in exterminating Jews, Gypsies, and homosexuals. General Eisenhower's visit to Auschwitz, walking among piles of corpses the Germans had no time to cremate, left the American Jews beside themselves trying to find news of their relatives. If they were fortunate to learn that their relatives had somehow escaped, the Americans were eager to send help, despite the impaired post war postal system.

My Uncle Béla and Aunt Sophie were trying to connect with their old Budapest employees, Jews and non- Jews, begging for information about our family. After many attempts, my Uncle Béla found a cutter from his dress salon. She reported that both my mother and father were killed at the Hidegség Concentration Camp, but I had survived and was living with the Winklers in our old apartment building on Eötvös Utca. The cutter also reported that my uncle's friends, the Schulzers, all survived thanks to their Christian maid who had hidden them during the Nazi occupation. Immediately, my uncle wrote to the Schulzers asking them to take me in until I could emigrate to the United States.

My aunt and uncle continued to search high and low to find a way to send me as much help as they could afford. It took them months, but one day my Aunt Sophie met a lady named Mrs. Kovács at the New York Hungarian Club on East 79th Street. It turned out that Mrs. Kovács was the mother of one Colonel Kovács, a United States army colonel who was in charge of the American Military Mission in Budapest! Mrs. Kovács had her ticket on the S.S. America for the first crossing of the Atlantic Ocean after the war. My aunt asked Mrs. Kovács for a BIG FAVOR!

"Would you agree to take two boxes as 'Accompanied Baggage' to Budapest along with you when you go on your trip?" she asked Mrs. Kovács. "We are trying to send some provisions to our nephew until he can get to America."

"Yes, indeed," answered Mrs. Kovács. "I would be happy to help."

This delighted my aunt and uncle who began to collect things to send to Budapest. They hired a professional shipping company, H.S. Dorf and Company, to build two "lifts" or boxes and started to fill them with goods (incidentally, my first job in the U.S. was with H.S. Dorf and Company on Broad Street, New York City).

Unfortunately, the unthinkable happened. On route across the Atlantic Ocean, Mrs. Kovács suffered a heart attack and died suddenly. The S.S. America docked at Le Havre, France, and the shipment mysteriously disappeared.

So, what was I doing for cash? In 1934, my family moved

from our big apartment at 81 Izabella Utca, to my grandmother's one-room apartment at 35 Eötvös Utca. We had more than a dozen very old, beautiful oriental carpets which we took with us. Knowing that I would not be able to take them with me to America, I made trips back to my old apartment where the Polish Jews were living to retrieve the carpets, and started selling them one after the other. By the time, I was ready to leave Budapest, my rugs were all gone.

Nine months later and just days away from leaving Russian-occupied Hungary for good, Mrs. Schulzer called to me,

"Endre, there is a card here from the Budapest Main Post Office asking for you to come pick up some packages."

Promptly I headed for the post office, card in hand. The clerk at the post office looked at my card and asked,

"Where did you park your truck?"

"Truck? What truck?" I answered. "I came to pick up my two packages."

"Well," he replied," Unless you're Hercules, you'll need a truck. One package is 1200 kilos and the other is 800 kilos. I doubt you can carry that all on your back."

I almost fainted. I rushed off to find my old friend, Winkler, who used to own a fruit and vegetable store.

"Lou, do you know where we can rent a horse and flatbed? I need to haul 2000 kilos!"

"No problem," he answered.

That afternoon we picked up the boxes, took them to the Schulzers, and unloaded them in the lobby because they would not fit on the elevator.

What had my aunt and uncle sent me? Everything that money could buy: cans of coffee, cans of lard, toothpaste, toothbrushes, suits, overcoats, shoes, boots, SPAM, canned hams, sardines, baked beans, jellies, jams, enough canned foods to feed an army!

Looking at the mountain of goods, I asked myself what in the world was I going to do with all this stuff five days before I was to leave Hungary? I could only do one thing. The most useful part of the shipment was money. In every jacket and pant pocket was an American fifty-dollar bill. I collected all the money, took an overcoat and one set of clothes. I would be traveling light. The rest of the stuff I left for the Schulzers and Winklers.

Had I received those boxes nine months earlier, I could have lived like a king. But they did symbolize how much my aunt and uncle loved me.

Much love, Grandpa

JANEK
March 7, 2010

Dear Andrew,

I was living with the Schulzers when Janek came to visit and discuss our futures. Janek, his sister, her husband and their ten-year-old son were Polish Jews who survived because they had false documents. During the German occupation, the Hungarian government had given them permission to move into my family's vacant apartment believing them to be Polish refugees fleeing from the advancing Russian Red Army.

Janek and I became fast friends. He spoke perfect Russian and now that the war was over, he had new false documents proving that he was a partisan fighter with the Russians. He had become friends with the Russian officers which proved to be very helpful.

Janek and his family were hoping to emigrate to Palestine, whereas I, by hook or crook, wanted to get to America to rejoin my Uncle Béla and Aunt Sophie

The first hurdle was how to escape from Hungary and cross the Russian invaders' "Iron Curtain" to Vienna, Austria. Janek thought he might be able to help because he knew a bunch of Russian officers whose job was to supply the Russian garrison in Vienna with food and tobacco. Sure enough, not too many weeks later, Janek reported that he had met a Russian major who agreed to smuggle me on his tobacco truck to Vienna for fifty dollars. That sounded like a good deal. I had a bunch of fifty dollar bills from my aunt and uncle's care package. In short time, I said goodbye to the Schulzers, Winklers, National University, and my law studies. With a small bag, I was ready for the trip.

Meanwhile, Janek had arranged for his own escape. We agreed that once we reached Vienna, we would meet at the Jewish Center, located at the Rothschild Hospital.

Everybody assured me that the trip would be a cake walk. The major had excellent documents straight from Russian headquarters in Budapest, and no one would dare to question such important orders coming from a high-ranking officer. How wrong they were!

Our truck stopped at the border station amidst a great deal of commotion. Orders were shouted that I did not understand. Trucks were moved left and right to be INSPECTED!

Russian NKVD (Secret Service Military Police) were in charge of border crossings. Although they were mostly women, they could order around even generals, never mind a major. After checking the major's documents, he was ordered to open the back of the truck. With bayonets affixed to their rifles, they started to stab the bales of tobacco behind which I was carefully packed. They were intently searching for contraband, stolen goods, stowaways, or anything else. Fortunately, I was back far enough in the truck so that their bayonets could not reach me. When they ordered the major to proceed, I peeked out and saw that his face had gone chalk white. He knew that had the NKVD found me, both he and I would have been shot with no questions asked.

The rest of the short trip was through pretty Austrian countryside, but having gone through living hell, I couldn't enjoy it very much. When I climbed out of the truck, I faced a gray, lifeless, hungry city unlike the one I had known before the war. It was a four-power (Russia, France, America and England) occupied city. Because the Russians were one of the occupiers, everything went downhill. There was no food anywhere. People were afraid to go outside because the Russians routinely harassed them and marched them to labor camps. Businesses were closed because there was nothing to sell. The few coffeehouses still open only served coffee or tea. There were no pastries for which Vienna was famous.

True to his word, Janek was waiting for me at the Rothschild Hospital. He happily reported that he had found a room with two beds for us on Praterstrasse, the main street connecting Vienna Center with the world-famous Prater Amusement Park which had claim to the first Ferris Wheel in Europe. As it turned out, finding an apartment for rent was not a big problem in Vienna. Finding something to eat was a whole different story. First, the retreating Germans cleaned everything out. If there were any crumbs left, the Russians took them. We passed most of our days trying to find anything to put in our mouths. The Rothschild Hospital had a soup line for the refugees where we could get a cup of soup.

I learned Jewish refugees were housed in the Rothschild Hospital. One could register there for emigration to several countries: U.S.A., Canada, Australia, or Palestine. I registered for the U.S.A. and was told that the wait was long. How long?

No one could tell, but we were talking years not months. This was discouraging news, but I, the eternal optimist, figured I could beat the odds. WRONG!

Meanwhile, Janek made friends with the Russian garrison and managed to get some travel papers for himself and me so that we could commute back to Budapest and get food before we both starved to death. I went back first and returned with some ham, duck, sausages, coffee, lard, and breads. Janek made the next trip. I don't recall a single meal in Vienna that was Viennese.

By going back and forth to Budapest, we were relatively well fed. But Vienna was still starving in the fall, so it was no big surprise when Janek came home one day with news that Berlin was on the verge of starvation. Some Russian soldiers returning to Vienna from Berlin informed Janek that people with food could make lots of money on the black market. Hungarian hams could especially be sold for super high prices.

This started Janek thinking as to how we could legally make a run to Berlin and make a ton of money. It all depended upon him securing Russian travel documents. We made the following plan: I was to bring hams back from Budapest while Janek worked on bribing some Russian officers to secure safe travel documents. This plan worked out okay, but it took several weeks. We feared the later we got to Berlin, the less valuable our food would be. We should not have worried.

Janek did a good job with the paperwork, and I stored up a treasure trove of food. The day finally arrived where we went to the Vienna main station and boarded the train to Berlin.

We prayed our travel documents were good. Since we could not read Russian, we had no idea how good they were until we were stopped the first time for a document check. Naturally, we were a bundle of nerves while the Russian Green Capped NKVD scrutinized first the content and then the authority who issued the travel papers. The process took several minutes in which we aged several years. Finally, the papers were stamped and shoved back to us. They must have been good papers because we were not ordered to disembark.

Traveling through the countryside was a shocking experience. The devastation from incessant bombings, artillery fire, and tank battles left the entire landscape in ruins. Where and how did people live? Mostly they were in underground bunkers and air raid shelters.

The trip on the train took much longer than scheduled. First, the tracks were frequently impassable, and the crew had to repair rails, track, and concrete sections. Second, Russian security kept stopping the train asking for travel documents. Sometimes they ordered people off the train, and this caused several arguments, shouting, cursing, and even fist fighting. Each and every incident gave us the shakes, but somehow we were always allowed to proceed. Janek and I never found out what our documents said, but whatever it was, it worked.

Approaching Berlin, the train slowed to a crawl. The engineer was extra careful as each train yard was vulnerable given the condition of the tracks. We expected to derail at any moment. Finally, the train came to a stop.

Stepping out of the railcar, we looked around, and as far

as we could see, there was not a building standing. It was a clear, bright day, and I estimated about ten kilometers of ruins starting from the station. Station? What station? There was not one brick left to the Berlin rail center.

We picked up our bags and started walking toward the city center. At first, there were no people that we could observe on the streets. Gradually, a few people showed up, then some more and even more. But all of them were females.

The Germans had recruited men as young as sixteen on up to defend Berlin. These were either killed or hauled to Russian labor camps. Military-aged men were all "swept" up by Russian security forces, never to see Germany again.

There was something unnerving about seeing only women. The way those women looked at us, we could tell they were missing absent husbands, fathers, brothers, and sons. We intentionally sped up our walking because we started to feel uncomfortable with all those women staring at us. But as evening was nearing, we needed to find a place to stay. We heard some nice piano music coming out of a shabby piano bar. The piano lady was quite attractive, and she offered to share her place with me. I gladly accepted and stayed with her for one week. She was extremely helpful in trying to bring us customers who were willing to pay us enormous sums of money for our food.

The experience of seeing Berlin in ruins gave me some satisfaction that the Germans got what they deserved. I was very grateful to the Allied soldiers who had sacrificed their lives, so that I could walk on the streets of Berlin that, not so long before, had been the capital of Europe.

Our trip back east to Vienna was fairly uneventful. There were fewer stops and passport controls. The atmosphere in the traveling compartments was much less fearful. It felt good to return to Vienna, and that's when we found out the basketful of Deutschmarks we had collected was next to worthless and that we had lost money on the trip instead of getting rich. Thankfully, we did not end up in a Russian labor camp [due to our good travel documents]. We only found out much later what an enormous risk we had taken.

Love, Grandpa

PARTING WAYS
March 23, 2010

Dear Andrew,

One day Janek came home all excited. The big tent circus was coming to the Prater! His excitement surprised me. Apparently, he had never seen a circus in Poland before. It was no big deal for me as I had been to many circuses with my cousins, but I went with him anyway for a change of scenery.

The circus was okay but nothing spectacular. That was until a dog act came out on stage. Eight to ten dogs performed amazing acrobatics. I had never seen anything like it in Budapest. An older fellow was the trainer, and the dogs obeyed him instantly. It was beautiful to watch. The audience loved it and applauded enthusiastically.

Janek didn't see any of it. He had eyes only for the trainer's assistant. She looked about twenty years old, had a model's figure, and a sweet, smiling face. She was picture perfect from head to toe.

As we were leaving, Janek went to the box office and bought two tickets for each of us, for the next five nights: first row, center aisle. At each of the next five performances, Janek sat with a bunch of red roses. When the act was over, he would get up, walk over to the pretty assistant, and with a big grin, hand her the roses. She would smile sweetly and thank him for the flowers.

On the fifth night, he handed her the roses with a note that read: "My name is Janek. I live at Praterstrasse 64, Apartment 5. I will be home from 2-4 p.m. each afternoon waiting for you to come. I hope to see you soon."

I laughed all the way home, telling Janek he was stupid to write her that note, but he was confident she would come. And she did. Many times, when I saw the light in the window, I would stay away from our room to give them privacy. I spent a lot of time walking the streets of Vienna and learning of its two-thousand-year-old history.

One evening when I returned home, Janek was excited because the dog lady had invited him and me for supper. Circus people made enough money to buy good food on the black market, so we were looking forward to a delicious, home cooked meal. We were not disappointed: meat, potatoes, dessert, wines, cognac, a veritable feast. We were stuffed for the first time in Vienna.

After dinner, we retired to the living room with coffee and brandy. The man (we didn't know if he was her father, boyfriend, or what?) told us how he had bought the dogs as puppies and trained them for eight years before they could perform perfectly on stage.

"They're really wolves," he said, "And have all the instincts of a wolf. Now if I gave them the command, 'Tear apart these two gentlemen,' within thirty seconds, there would not be a bone left of you."

With that said, he took a big sip of his coffee.

For some reason, I became very uncomfortable listening to this guy. He didn't exhibit any emotion. He had told his little story quite matter-of-factly. I couldn't tell if he was serious or just pulling our legs. In any case, I'd had enough. I pulled on Janek's sleeve and made the excuse that we had to go because my train to Budapest was leaving early in the morning. We said thank you and were out of there in a flash. When we got out on the street, I said to Janek, "You can fool around if you wish, but I'm moving out of the apartment."

Janek answered, "I'm no fool. I got the message loud and clear. From now on, I'm calling it quits."

And he did.

By going back and forth to Budapest, I was able to get enough food to survive for a while. It was disturbing, however, that the Jewish refugees in Vienna were not going anywhere, but kept waiting and waiting for visas with no success. The rumor at the Rothschild Hospital was that visas were more likely to be obtained in U.S. occupied Germany, but not in Austria.

Meanwhile, I met a nice, Viennese girl at the Rothschild Hospital. She was a nursing student who was quite pretty and very intelligent. She knew a lot of history, and I learned so much from her. She showed me some of the loveliest parts of Vienna, but she would never enter the Russian Zone. She had heard too many horror stories about Russian behavior. I genuinely got to like her, even love her, but I respected her too much to do more than kiss her.

One day when I returned to our room with bags of food from a Budapest trip, what did I find? Janek was in bed with my girlfriend!

"You dirty scum!" I yelled. "You have the nerve to shack up with your friend's girl!"

"I did you a favor," he insisted.

"Really? And what kind of favor was that?" I demanded.

"I was concerned that you would give up joining your relatives in New York and that you would be stuck in Vienna for the rest of your life. I only wanted to help you decide to continue your journey west to America," argued Janek.

"That you did!" I replied angrily.

Love, Grandpa

QUOTAS
April 12, 2010

Dear Andrew,

The year was 1945. The war in Europe was over and the cleanup had begun. It was a big job because most of Europe was practically in ruins. The bridges, rail lines, and communication networks had all been destroyed or severely damaged. Thousands of homes were destroyed that left many people living underground in bunkers or bomb shelters. You wouldn't know it if you traveled in Europe today, but in 1945...

And then there was the human cost. Though the German Nazis and their willing allies succeeded in destroying about six million Jewish lives, there were survivors like me. Hundreds of thousands of Jews were wandering around Europe looking for a new home because they refused to go back from where they originally came. Who wanted to go back to a country where they had intended to kill you? So where should they go? Governments agreed that they needed a place to live but, "Not in my backyard!" After all, these were Jews.

Perhaps they should all go to Palestine where they lived for thousands of years. That resulted in a loud outcry from the Arabs, who thought that a Jewish immigration would threaten their nomadic way of life. What about Australia? It was a great, empty, expanse of a continent. Well, Australia did admit a limited few who had relatives living there. Canada? Also, practically empty with only twenty million people at that time.

A few went there as well. Then came the" biggie," the U.S.A.

Like President Franklin Roosevelt before him, President Harry Truman insisted on not meddling with the antiquated, pre-war quota system. No changes could be authorized. The country was already full, brimming to the seams, with an untenable population of one hundred forty million in 1945 (It did grow to over three hundred million by 2014, but not because of the Jews).

Harry Truman was ambivalent toward Jews. He didn't have anything against them since he had a Jewish partner in his haberdashery shop for a number of years. But he was also not fond of them. A story I read about Harry Truman went like this:

One day, his Jewish partner said to Harry, "Harry, you and I have been partners for years, yet you never once invited me to your house in all this time. How come?"

"Joe," Truman replied, "My mother-in-law (Bess's mother with whom they lived) would not allow a Jew in her home."

Truman never minced words. He always told you the way things were.

In addition to his own feelings, there was great pressure from the Labor Unions to whom, one could argue, Truman owed his political career. The unions viewed skilled, educated immigrants as unwanted, low-wage competition. And so, Truman listened.

Due to the tight quota system, I was forced to wait my turn in Germany for two years. I was lucky because some of my friends waited for three or more. Rules were rules. By contrast, after the unsuccessful 1955 Hungarian Revolution, President Eisenhower scrapped the quota system, threw open the border, and allowed every Hungarian (primarily Christian) to migrate to America whether or not they had relatives in the U.S. They needed sponsors, but the Christian churches in the U.S. sponsored everyone who applied.

Much love, Grandpa

MUNICH TO FRANKFURT
April 18, 2010

Dear Andrew,

After my falling out with Janek, and the end of our friendship, my thinking turned toward the west. I needed to plan my next move.

Despite daily trips to the Jewish Center at the Rothschild Hospital, I had not learned of a single success story of anyone getting a visa to the U.S., Canada, Australia, or Palestine.

Days earlier, I had gotten an invitation out of the blue to join my so-called cousin, Nick Rochlitz. I had stayed friends with Nick since Debrecen days and had even been the best man at his wedding in Budapest. Actually, it had been a double wedding because Nick married Rose, and Nick's best friend married Rose's younger sister. Now the two couples lived in a D.P. (Displaced Persons) camp near Munich, Germany.[15] I had no idea that they escaped Hungary. Nick wrote that he had come down with tuberculosis and had been transferred to a hospital. However, Rose, her sister, and brother-in-law, were staying at the camp. Nick promised there would be plenty of food. I quietly packed my bag in Vienna, and without saying anything to Janek, I took the streetcar to the railroad station and took the night train from Vienna to Munich. I never saw Janek again.

---

15 "From 1945 to 1952, more than 250,000 Jewish displaced persons (DPs) lived in camps and urban centers in Germany, Austria, and Italy" (United States Holocaust Memorial Museum, "Displaced Persons").

Munich was in the American zone; therefore, life was closer to normal. The CARE packages from the American Jews were actually delivered to the D.P. camp inhabitants (I suspected CARE packages to Vienna went directly to the black market as the intended never saw any aid). There was good medical care and the camp was located at the base of the alps, a beautiful setting. Various aid agencies maintained the D. P. Camps which consisted of shacks, communal bathrooms, and kitchens which produced good nutritious food.

Nick was still at the TB hospital, but Rose was happy to see me. She was a sweet, hospitable, kind person in spite of the routine and boring camp life. All our physical needs were well taken care of, but nothing was going on. We had freedom to go in and out of the camp, but with the way we all felt about Germans, no one had the desire to go out. I searched everywhere in the camp looking for Budapest Jews who I might know: Boy Scouts? schoolmates perhaps? But I couldn't find a single one. Did they all get killed? The thought made me very depressed.

Everything was perfect, except people kept moving in, and nobody was moving out. Horace Greely said one hundred years earlier, "Go West, young man. Go West," and that become my motto too. I finally met a Hungarian Jew, not from Budapest but from the countryside. He had survived a concentration camp and was now preparing to move to Frankfurt.

"What's in Frankfurt?" I asked.

"Oh, that's where all the big Jewish agencies are and where people get visas," he answered.

"VISAS!" I jumped as if struck by lightning.

"Yes, you need to get to Frankfurt if you're serious about leaving Europe," he advised.

"I'm going to Frankfurt," I announced to Rose who immediately started to cry.

"I hate to leave you here, but in a few weeks, Nick will be well and all of you will be moving toward Palestine, your final destination. Wait and see. You'll be moving to the Jewish homeland."

That calmed her down a little bit. I packed up my few things, kissed them all goodbye, and left for the train station.

Frankfurt was a big city but badly damaged during the war. Lots and lots of ruins everywhere; not much car traffic, but many streetcars and buses. If Berlin was the German Washington D.C., Frankfurt was the New York City equivalent. There was a vitality in Frankfurt I had not seen anywhere in Germany.

The two Jewish agencies were the AJDC (American Joint Distribution Committee) and the HIAS (Hebrew Immigration Aid Society). Because the AJDC building was much bigger and seemed more professional, I chose it to help me with my needs.

They gave me some money to go and eat something while they looked for a place for me to stay. When I returned after lunch, they were happy to report that a Dagi Singer from Budapest had one extra bed that he would rent me. The address was Heligkruez Strasse 10, not far from AJDC headquarters.

Dagi was living in the apartment of Frau Theiss, a war

widow, and her fourteen-year-old son. He rented the bedroom which had two beds, and Frau Theiss and her son slept in the kitchen.

Dagi was still in bed when I went to claim my sleeping place after lunch.

"There is nothing for me to do," he said. "Besides, I'm really hungry and it's better to not burn up a lot of calories."

The next day I went to the AJDC for registration. They asked me a lot of questions: What was my background? Why did I want to go to America and not Palestine? What schooling did I have? Where did I learn such good English? (After my aunt and uncle had left for America, my mother had traded home-cooked meals for lessons with an English-speaking tutor for three years). After checking German transport records from Hungary, they discovered my name on the Bergen Belsen[16] list (the Germans' intended destination for me had I not escaped) and stamped my application accordingly. This put me ahead of the general list, but still not until the end of 1947 for going to America.

It wasn't long before I was staying in bed at least half the day, because the care packages that the American Jews kept sending never made it to Heligkreuz Strasse, but also went straight to the black market. For some reason, there were two things that we did receive and that saved us from starvation: bread and sugar. We poured sugar on slices of bread and that was breakfast and lunch. We had nothing to eat for dinner.

16 Bergen-Belsen was a Nazi concentration camp in northern Germany. Anne Frank, whose diary became a bestseller, was among the 50,000 who died there (United States Holocaust Memorial Museum, "Bergen-Belsen").

Needless to say, we lost a lot of weight.

Time in Frankfurt, Germany, slowed down for me considerably. Here I was, twenty years old, dying to go to America, get my life on track for the future, and rejoin my aunt and uncle whom I hadn't seen for six years. I was full of dreams, ambitions, and pent- up energy. I was languishing with my roommate, Dagi, going nowhere fast.

We had regular farewell parties for the lucky ones who obtained long-awaited visas to faraway places: America, Canada, Australia, and Palestine. We watched them pack their bags, and we accompanied them to the train station. Don't get me wrong; I'm not talking about a flood of people leaving, rather a trickle. But there was movement, and it was in the right direction!

A couple things made our lives a little more bearable. Dagi and I had girlfriends. Frankfurt was the birthplace of my big love affair. I met a Hungarian Jewish girl, Eve Brenner, at the ADJC office. Eve and her mother had survived Auschwitz, but her father had died there. The Jewish agencies were allocated a number of uniformed office workers, so Eve wore an American army uniform. This allowed her entrance to the PX (Post Exchange). For the first time, I got to taste American style ice cream. What a difference! Eve was an intellectual. She was a voracious reader; her favorites being history and literature. Because she was a regular worker, she earned a salary. She and her mother lived in a nice apartment and fed me from time to time, for which I was grateful. Eve had applied to move to Australia where her mother's brother lived in Melbourne.

She was ready and willing to switch her destination to New York, if I ever got there and found a way for the two of us to support ourselves (Unfortunately, it took me until 1957 before I earned one thousand dollars a month and by then we had drifted apart).

Some of Dagi's and my friends were transferred to various Displaced Person Camps near Frankfurt. He and I would take the train to go visit them. There were also a number of hot baths and sulfur baths surrounding Frankfurt which had survived the war unscathed. They reflected the old-world charm and elegance that was difficult to find in post war Germany. We went to Bad Hamburg and Bad Neuheim to get a break from living in dreary Frankfurt. The slow pace of people moving out and migrating was frustrating.

It was the summer of 1947, when FINALLY, I received a postcard from the American Consulate in Frankfurt requesting I present myself for PROCESSING! No fuss, no bell ringing, the postcard was addressed Heilgkreuz Strasse 10 and was postmarked the day before. Breathlessly, I rushed to the Consulate where they had a pile of papers for me to sign. I had to answer questions like, "Were you ever a communist?" Are you kidding? I almost lost my life crossing the "Iron Curtain" trying to escape communism.

When I finally passed all the interrogations, I was escorted to the transportation desk. In addition to my visa, I was given a steamship ticket (already prepaid by my uncle) on the S.S. Marine Flasher, sailing from Bremerhaven on October 29th and arriving in New York on November 10, 1947.

I went outside where the sun shone brightly in the clear blue sky. I sat down on the front steps and cried. I cried and cried as a big weight was lifted from my shoulders. Was it really possible that my fervent dream was about to become reality? How much I had endured to reach this point in my life: running, hiding, escaping, starving, and the pain of losing both my parents and many other loved ones. Was this the end, and also the beginning, of my bright new promising future?

Love, Grandpa

ONBOARD TO AMERICA
April 20, 2010

Dear Andrew,

The trip to America on a converted troop ship was anything but pleasant. The date was November 1947, and the Atlantic Ocean was in a foul mood. Waves, between twenty and thirty feet high, got the ship climbing up tall mountains, and rocked it from left to right on the way down. Ninety percent of the passengers were seasick.

I was one of the few who showed up in the mess hall. I was so starved that absolutely nothing, not even fifty foot waves, could keep me away from food. The food was good and plentiful because so few people were able to eat. There was a black steward who sort of attached himself to me. I was an oddity because I was able to eat non-stop, from morning to night. Everything I asked for, from steak to strawberries, the steward delivered promptly. He sat next to me and watched me eat and eat. He said that never in his entire life had he seen anyone eat so much. Of course, he never saw anyone starve that much either. I was it.

Between bites, I managed to ask him to fill me in on life in America. I was very curious to learn everything I could about my new country. The steward was obliging, and he started to talk about what life was like for BLACK PEOPLE in 1947 America. I was shocked, and almost choked on my food, when I heard that blacks were only allowed to ride in the back of the bus, that they were not allowed to eat in the "Whites Only" section, that they were forced to pee in separate bathrooms, and that they were totally segregated in schools!

You must remember that I was coming from a country where we never saw any black people, so this kind of black prejudice was completely alien to me. In my mind, I had always pictured America as a land of milk and honey for ALL people. I never expected this kind of racial prejudice. All this should not have surprised me. Since eight years of age, I had avidly read all the Mark Twain books, so I should have known. Somehow, it had not registered on me as reality. In my child's mind, I had read the Uncle Tom story as fiction. But America was real and its racism deadly.

Life for Jews in the United States was no picnic either. The Klu Klux Klan declared they hated Jews, Negroes, and Catholics in that order. Jews were restricted from being members or gaining admission in many places: country clubs, athletic clubs, hotels, and restaurants in New York City. Posted signs read, "No Jews or dogs allowed." And then there were the quotas on Jews. Harvard, Princeton, Yale and Columbia all had a ten percent limit on Jewish admission. When I applied to New York University in 1948, they said I didn't have the right high school diploma. I not only had the right diploma, I had also completed one year of Law School in Budapest. Many years later in 1971, the University of Chicago Graduate School of Business admitted me with no questions asked.

Prejudices existed against others too. [Historically] there was prejudice against the Irish, a lot of heckling of Italians, and the granddaddy of racial hatred, of course, was the killing of the Indians (Native Americans) together with the buffalo. Our "melting pot" has some cracks in it, that's for sure. Yet, no one has a better or more perfect melting pot than we do.

Since I was so bitterly hated, and nearly killed because of racism, I decided then and there to devote my life to assist those who were underprivileged and in need of a helping hand. I tried to help those who helped others, such as being on the board of a charitable hospital or helping to raise funds for needy and deserving students at the University of Chicago where I had received my MBA. I feared that I didn't do enough. Of course, if I convinced my children and grandchildren to help those in need, I would be happy in the knowledge that my teachings had adherents. "Help" can take many forms: outright gifts of money, food and clothing; lending an ear or a shoulder to cry on; making a phone call to make a person feel good; or offering advice when a person feels lost. You and I were Boy Scouts, so we know what is expected of us. Just follow their teachings.

Much love, Grandpa

ARRIVAL
May 1, 2010

Dear Andrew,

The ship from Germany arrived in New York City late in the evening and docked overnight, not far from the Statue of Liberty. It was held there for twelve hours in "quarantine." If there were passengers with communicable diseases, they would be spotted and removed.

We couldn't see Manhattan from where we were parked, but we could see Staten Island. The traffic that we saw surprised me. All night long, cars ran non-stop in one direction and the other. "Don't these people ever sleep," I wondered. We had never seen anything like that in Europe. Curiosity and happiness that we had finally arrived kept us from going below to catch some sleep. We were on the deck the entire night. Loudspeakers constantly warned the passengers not to bunch up on one side of the ship, for fear of tipping over. But who wanted to be on the "wrong" side, looking at the black water, when you could watch the highway and lights of Staten Island and the good old U.S.A. on the other side?

The ship lifted anchor and very slowly, almost majestically, we started out toward Manhattan Island. The many lights around me started to dim as the sliver of sun arose in the eastern sky. With that, our view broadened and we were finally able to take a good look at the "Promised Land." Lower Manhattan, Battery Park, and Wall Street, with all their skyscrapers were breathtaking. This was the first time I had seen skyscrapers. In Hungary, and all over Europe, most buildings were only four stories tall. Only cathedrals were tall enough to push their crosses up to the sky. Seeing the tall buildings filled me with awe. Little did I know that in a few weeks, I would be running all around in between those tall monuments as a messenger for a shipping company.

There was busy traffic in the harbor: barges cruising up and down the Hudson River, ferryboats crossing between Staten Island and lower Manhattan, occasionally, big ocean liners being towed toward their Manhattan piers. There was lots of movement, lots of color, and lots of activity. At this moment, however, I was just overcome with awe and joy at the anticipation of being reunited with my Uncle Béla and Aunt Sophie after an absence of six years! Last time they saw me, I was just a little older than Levi [Andrew's thirteen-year-old brother], and now I was a twenty-year-old grown man.

I pushed toward the ship's railings trying to get a glimpse of my aunt and uncle, but it was impossible to spot them amidst the heaving crowd of fellow passengers, most of whom were also looking forward to reuniting with their loved ones after many years of absence. Would they recognize me? Would they open their home for me? What would become of me? I confess, I was anxious, but excited and happy that I had made it to America ALIVE. If that wasn't a miracle, what was? As to recognizing me, I need not have feared. When our ship gently pivoted, with the help of tugboats, into its berth at Pier 64, North River (Hudson River), my uncle was eagerly trying to find me among the hundreds of refugees who mobbed the upper deck. Scanning the multitude of people on deck, he suddenly spotted his pigeon-gray winter coat that he had sent to me in Budapest.

"There is my winter coat!" he cried out to my aunt, who was stretching her neck to search through the crowd on deck. "There is Endre!"

The coat I wore was one of the gifts that had come to Budapest in the two big boxes. It was one of the few things I smuggled out when I escaped from Russian-occupied Hungary to Vienna, Austria.

Debarking was fairly swift and easy. As I stepped off the gangplank, I joyfully thought, "I AM AN AMERICAN!" After a brief search, I found my uncle and aunt. Unashamedly, we cried. We hugged and cried. Forgetting about luggage and everything else, we were in our own little world overcome with emotion.

"I promised your parents," my uncle said through his tears, "that when the war was over, I would bring you to America. Thank the LORD that at least you survived. Now you're safe and at home!"

A big stone fell off my shoulders. I was wanted and loved.

Much love, Grandpa

EPILOGUE

"Taxi, Taxi!" my Uncle Béla shouted.

"What? We need a taxi? I thought everyone in America owned a car," I said much surprised.

"No," Uncle Béla replied, "We don't own a car. You'll find we have excellent public transportation in New York, and if that isn't enough, we can always find a taxi."

This was pretty disappointing to me, and I vowed that one day I would have a car.

The taxi drove us east to Park Avenue, then north to 79th Street. My aunt and uncle lived at 229 East 79th Street, midtown, east-side Manhattan. It didn't take us long to get there as the traffic was very light after the war.

"We're home," announced my uncle.

"What are all those ugly ladders in front of the building?" I asked.

"Those are fire-escapes. They are ladders so that the firemen can climb up a burning building," my aunt replied.

"Do they really need those? They are so ugly," I insisted.

"They save lives," my uncle explained.

Up we went in the elevator, all the way to the fifteenth floor. I was awestruck by the view as we entered the apartment. From the living room window, I could see south all the way to the Statue of Liberty. The apartment had two bedrooms and a maid's quarters. I lived in the maid's quarters just off the kitchen, which had its own bathroom and separate entrance, until I got married in 1958. The only exception was when I was drafted into the army for two years of military service and was stationed in Virginia and Germany.

I really enjoyed, no, I LOVED New York! New York in those days was a city of walk-ups and neighborhoods. Starting from 79th Street, I could walk through neighborhoods with their many different nationalities, unique traditions, cultures, and exceptional food; 79th Street was Hungarian, 72nd Street was Czechoslovakian, and 86th Street was German. Where else could one experience such variety, all within walking distance?

I received a big surprise when my uncle told me that a job was already waiting for me. Not a great job, but a job where I would earn money. On one hand, I was happy that my aunt and uncle provided me with a sense of purpose. On the other hand, I was hoping for a little time to unwind after all that I had gone through. Oh, well! I was a messenger at H. S. Dorf and Company, 89th and Broad Street, in the shadow of the New York Stock Exchange. I was paid $27.50 a week, with $15.00 a week going to my aunt for room and board.

My job was to take custom documents to the steamship companies, and back to our office, non-stop. That first winter in New York, we suffered the biggest snowfall. I had to climb over the roofs of cars to cross the streets. What an experience! I made lots of friends in the business and became something like a "fixer" [problem solver]. Promotions came frequently, and by the end of the third year in the business, I was promoted to Import Traffic Manager for the American Shipping Company, just behind the U.S. Customs House, where I made $75.00 per week. That job ended when I was drafted by the U.S. Army at the end of the Korean War in 1954. My background and work experience in the transportation business landed me an assignment to the Transportation Training Command in Fort Eustis, Virginia, where I met my good friend and future brother-in-law, Philip Crane, from Chicago, Illinois.

Returning to civilian life, after my two-year military career, my uncle, once again, had a job all lined up where I was paid $200 per week! The job turned out to be quite painful due to a personality clash with the president. I was sorry to leave my job with its offices on the 69th floor of the Empire State Building. From the apartment on 79th Street, my aunt could watch for my office light to go off, and she would know to start heating my dinner.

I was lucky to get my next job with Kurt Orban Company [from 1957-1980] at Exchange Place in Jersey City. It was a steel import company where I eventually rose to Director and Vice President of Midwestern sales. The pay was sufficient enough to start thinking about marriage.

After having met my army buddy's younger sister, Judy, who had accompanied her dad to New York on a business trip, I fell head over heels in love. On May 1st, 1958, we got married in the Park Avenue Methodist Church, with the Reverend's wife and the Head Church Usher as our only witnesses.

We were blessed with four sons and one daughter, but tragedy struck when we lost our son Jamie shortly before his fourth birthday from a rare autoimmune disease. Nothing can match the pain of losing one of your children!

Our big family was eventually enriched by two daughters-in-law, one son-in-law, and eleven grandchildren, one more loving than the other. Judy and I, now in our eighties, can rightfully thank the LORD for a good and productive life.

Over the seventy-plus years since the end of World War II, many people have commented (some even complimented) about how I had apparently recovered so seamlessly after the Holocaust. They came to this conclusion because they only saw my outer skin. If they had x-ray vision, they would have known differently. Since eight of my small, close-knit family of eleven had perished, I was a broken, angry, troubled young man. Then two survivors, my Aunt Olga Rochlitz and my Uncle Sándor Lustig, lost their minds and soon after passed away from grief. I realized that I could not allow my deep hurt and broken heart to control me. I had to gather all my inner strength and pull down my personal "Iron Curtain." I refused to let my thoughts reminisce about my parents, my cousins, and my childhood. All these memories had to be walled off. For over fifty years, I refused to look back, to remember the good times, or to feel the warmth of my mother and father's affections. They no longer existed.

My Uncle Béla and Aunt Sophie Rosenthal (who Americanized their name to Ross) devoted their lives to make me comfortable and to help me forget. Without their overwhelming love, kindness, support, and generosity, my outcome would have been altogether different. When I arrived in New York with my little suitcase and virtually no change of clothing, they immediately took me to Barney's where I got outfitted from head to toe in new clothes to begin my life as a New Yorker. My aunt and uncle did not have children of their own, so in their minds they adopted me, and I became their son [and legally changed my name to Andrew Ross]. They made all the difference in the world to me.

After about fifty years, I slowly permitted myself to look back. Oh, how much joy and ache came at the same time: visiting and playing with my cousins, the Jewish festivities in my cousins' large apartment, my family's trip to Monte Carlo where a photographer took a picture of me holding the hand of my white-uniformed governess on the steps of the famous casino, the time I got scared when the train entered a dark Swiss tunnel and another train loudly passed going the opposite direction, our family trips to beautiful Lake Balaton in our chauffeur-driven Horch limousine where we would swim and enjoy the colorful sailboats.

As I kept opening cracks of my memory, I realized what a happy childhood I had even when we became poor and our lives changed so quickly. I will never forget my tenth birthday. My mother and father bought me one ticket to the opera house to see Puccini's Tosca. I do not remember why or what caused it, but my father and I got into a bad argument. As a result, I tore the precious opera ticket into many little pieces. My father stayed up all night trying to paste the ticket back together. The next day I was able to see wonderful Tosca. You might ask, why did they only buy one ticket? Because that is all the money they had.

Now that I am an old man, I permit myself an "open door" policy. I allow myself to think more and more about our family. I discover memories that I thought I had lost, and it brings a smile to my face and an ache to my heart at the same time. I feel that I have succeeded. I was able to do things only "normal" people could achieve. But then comes a reality check. The reality is that at eighty-nine years of age, I still bleed on the inside.

Among the papers I was able to bring with me to America, there is a letter. The letter is from my father. It is a goodbye letter, the last words my father was able to leave for me. As of today, I am still not able to open it and read it. I know when I get the courage, my heart will bleed all over again.

Andrew Ross (Endre Lövinger)
September 2016

TIME LINE

1863 Grandmother Fanny Bock Rosenthal Darvas is born

SEPTEMBER 5, 1893 Josef Lövinger is born

JULY 27, 1899 Erna Rosenthal is born

1914-1919 World War I
Collapse of the Austro-Hungarian Empire

AUGUST 1926 Erna Rosenthal and Josef Lövinger are married

JULY 21, 1927 Endre Matyas Laslo Lövinger is born

1933 Josef Lövinger goes bankrupt- family moves in with Grandmother Fanny
Adolf Hitler becomes Chancellor of Germany

1939 World War II begins
Germans occupy Austria (less than 200 miles from Budapest)

1941 Uncle Béla and Aunt Sophie Rosenthal depart for America.
Grandmother Fanny dies

Pearl Harbor Attack-U.S.A. enters WWII

MARCH 19,1944 Germans invade Hungary
JUNE 1944 D-Day Invasion

July 20, 1944 Assassination attempt on Hitler fails

OCTOBER 19, 1944 Endre Lövinger and Uncle Sándor Lustig are rounded up and taken to Labor Camp by Arrow Cross

OCTOBER 29, 1944 Endre Lövinger escapes on Elizabeth Bridge. Josef and Erna Lövinger are taken by Arrow Cross and begin "Death March" to Hidegség Concentration Camp.

NOVEMBER 1944 Lou Winkler sneaks Endre into the Hungarian Work Brigade for Jewish Men. Endre and Lou escape from Work Brigade. Endre moves in with Tuscháks and begins forced labor loading barges for Germans.

DECEMBER 1944 Josef Lövinger dies in Hidegség Concentration Camp. Erna Lövinger and Aunt Sándorné Lustig are executed by firing squad near Hidegség Concentration Camp. German S.S. order Endre to decorate Christmas tree at S.S. headquarters.

JANUARY 1945 Russian army invades Budapest

APRIL 30, 1945 Adolf Hitler commits suicide

MAY 8, 1945 Germany surrenders

OCTOBER 7, 1947 Endre Lövinger receives visa to United States in Frankfurt, Germany

OCTOBER 29, 1947 Endre Lövinger departs Bremerhaven, Germany for United States

NOVEMBER 11, 1947 Endre Lövinger arrives in America

REFERENCES

ArchiveAuthor. "'Death March' of 50,000 Hungarian Jews Described at Eichmann Trial." *Jewish Telegraphic Agency.* June 2, 1961. Accessed April 9, 2017. http://www.jta.org/1961/06/02/archive/death-march-of-50000-hungarian-jews-described-at-eichmann-trial/amp.

Benyoseph, Kati Tuschák. Personal Interview with the Author. May 21. 2017.

"Claus Von Stauffenberg." *Jewish Virtual Library: a Project of Aice*, Jewish Virtual Library. Accessed May 21, 2017. www.jewishvirtuallibrary.org/claus-von-stauffenberg.

"Introduction: Budapest 1944-2014." *Yellow-Star Houses*, www.yellowstarhouses.org/historical_background/introduction. Accessed 6 June 2017.

Kershaw, Alex. *The Envoy: The Epic Rescue of the Jews of Europe in the Desperate Closing Months of World War II.* Waterville, Me.: Thorndike, 2010.

Lambert, Sean. "The Horthy Era (1920–1944)." *The Orange Files.* February 25, 2017. Accessed April 9, 2017. https://theorangefiles.hu/the-horthy-era-1920-1944-long/.

Levéltár, Magyar Zsidó. "Hidegség, 1944. November és 1945. Március." *Digitális Konfliktus Adatbázis.* Társaldami Kofliktusok. Accessed May 21, 2017.

Snowy Elisabeth Bridge, 1940. Digital image. *Vintage Everyday*. N.p., 29 Apr. 2016. Web. 5 June 2017. <http://www.vintag.es/2016/04/amazing-vintage-pictures-show-change-of.html>.

"The Holocaust: Forced Labor." *Jewish Virtual Library: a Project of Aice*, Jewish Virtual Library, Accessed May 21, 2017. www.jewishvirtuallibrary.org/forced-labor-in-the-holocaust. United States Holocaust Memorial Museum. "Bergen-Belsen." *Holocaust Encyclopedia*. Accessed April 9, 2017. https://www.ushmm.org/wlc/en/article.php?ModuleId=10005224.

United States Holocaust Memorial Museum. "Displaced Persons." *Holocaust Encyclopedia*. Accessed April 9, 2017. https://www.ushmm.org/wlc/en/article.php?ModuleId=10005462.

United States Holocaust Memorial Museum. "Jewish Population of Europe in 1933: Population Data by Country." Accessed May 21, 2017. https://www.ushmm.org/wlc/en/article.php?ModuleId=10005161.

View from the Royal Palace in Spring 1945. Digital image. *Interview with General Karl Pfeffer-Wildenbach, Commander of the 'Budapest Fortress'*. Daily Historical Sources, 16 Feb. 2016. Web. 5 June 2017. <http://napitortenelmiforras.blog.hu/2016/02/16/interju_a_tabornokkal_karl_pfeffer-wildenbruch_a_budapest-erod_parancsnoka>.

ACKNOWLEDGEMENTS

First, I would like to thank my son Andrew for his willingness to make his personal treasures from his grandpa public.

Many thanks also for the unconditional love and support of our spouses, Judy Ross and David Oury.

To Shannon Ishizaki, Denise Meister, Kaeley Dunteman, and Lauren Blue of TEN16 Press, my utmost gratitude for your guidance, enthusiasm, and genuine hearts.

Without the technical wizardry from Hannah Oury, Rachael Oury, Lillie Ross, and Kim Hevrdejs, I would have given up long ago.

Much appreciation for translation help from Kati Tuschák Benyoseph and background information from Yoram Gordon.

Matthew Ross, Peter Ross, John Ross, Rochelle Witter, and Carol Kuehl were so very kind to read the manuscript and give helpful input.

Jonathan Oury, thank you for your understanding and patience with your very distracted mother. Levi Oury, without you, the idea of writing Grandpa's story would have remained an idea and would have never gone further.

Words cannot express the love, respect, and gratitude I have toward my father, Andrew Ross. My heart is still tender from losing him suddenly just two months after he finished writing the Epilogue. Dad, I think you would be pleased with how this book turned out.

And finally, I would like to thank you, dear reader, for your interest and curiosity in the world you inhabit. May you be a shining light to the lives around you.

Sincerely, Deborah Erna Oury

www.ingramcontent.com/pod-product-compliance
Lightning Source LLC
Chambersburg PA
CBHW051651040426
42446CB00009B/1084